The
First
90
Days
in Government

Critical Success Strategies for
New Public Managers at All Levels

Peter H. Daly
Michael Watkins

with Cate Reavis

Harvard Business School Press
Boston, Massachusetts

978-1-59139-955-1 (ISBN 13)
Library of Congress Cataloging-in-Publication Data

Daly, Peter H., 1941–
   The first 90 days in government : critical success strategies for new public
managers at all levels / Peter H. Daly and Michael Watkins with Cate Reavis.
        p. cm.
   Includes bibliographical references and index.
   ISBN 1-59139-955-6
   1.   Public administration—United States.   2.   Civil service—United States.
I. Title: First ninety days in government. II. Watkins, Michael, 1956– III. Reavis,
Cate. IV. Title.
JK421.D34 2006
352.3—dc22

                                                            2005034063

Contents

Conclusion: Accelerate Everyone 225

The approach as a whole. Seeing the forest *and* the trees. Striving to accelerate yourself and everyone in your organization.

Preface

Our work on this book actually began in the early 1990s, when Peter was leading change in senior executive positions in the federal bureaucracy and Michael was a freshly minted assistant professor at Harvard's Kennedy School of Government studying change in public- and private-sector organizations, including one that Peter was leading. After the study ended, we stayed in touch and became friends, all the while continuing to talk about the challenges confronting leaders in the public sector. Even after Michael moved on to the Harvard Business School and became focused on private-sector leadership transitions, our discussions continued. This book is the result of that fruitful dialogue.

During his thirty-three-year career in government, more than half of it spent as a senior executive, Peter interviewed many candidates for supervisory and management positions. In these interviews, after suggesting that the candidate assume for the moment that he or she had been selected, he would ask, "What would you do upon reporting to your new position?" Unsurprisingly, the answers varied widely. They ranged from the astute, those who clearly had thought about why they wanted the job and how they were going to approach it, to the clueless, who often gave unintentionally humorous replies such as, "I wouldn't do anything for two months." In between were many cases of honest befuddlement, even from candidates who had impressive backgrounds, but who lacked a systematic way of approaching the new leadership role they were seeking. Particularly at sea were those who were entering the government environment for the first time, perhaps coming from a career in business or at a nonprofit, and were seemingly unaware of the gulf that separated the two managerial continents of the public and private sectors. So when we began discussing writing this book together, Peter knew there was an opportunity to help future public-sector leaders better prepare to take their new positions.

The goal of this book is to provide you, the reader, with a framework for understanding and successfully meeting the challenges you will face in your first few months in your new leadership position in government. Why do you need this framework? Because transition periods are critical times when small differences in your actions can have disproportionate effects on your later success. Regardless of level, leaders in government are vulnerable in their first few months in new positions because they lack detailed knowledge of the challenges they will face and what it will take to succeed in meeting them. Failure to gain momentum during your transition period virtually guarantees an uphill battle for the rest of your tenure at the job. Success in building credibility and securing some early wins, on the other hand, lays a foundation for longer-term success.

If you are reading this, you likely are either in the midst of a transition to a new leadership role in government, are about to start one, or are aspiring to become a leader in the future. In any case, this book will equip you with strategies and tools to get up to speed and to achieve more sooner. You will learn how to diagnose your situation and gain clarity about its risks and opportunities. You will assess your strengths and weaknesses and identify your greatest personal vulnerabilities in your new situation. You will gain insights into how to learn about your new organization and establish your priorities more quickly. You will learn how to diagnose and align the strategy, structure, systems, skills, and culture of your new organization. Perhaps most importantly, you will get solid advice about how to manage key relationships by building teams, creating alliances, and recruiting a supportive network of advisers and counselors. Use this book as a road map for creating your transition plan. If you do, you will get up to speed, and help others do so, faster than you thought possible.

This book draws on the research and conclusions contained in *The First 90 Days: Critical Success Strategies for New Leaders at All Levels,* Michael's best-selling transition guide. But the differences between the private and public sectors of management are so deep and significant that direct translation of ideas simply wasn't possible. The premises, analyses, and suggested strategies contained in this edition are therefore based primarily on direct research with an outstanding group of career public executives who were kind enough to participate in extensive interviews conducted by Cate; those interviews were then interpreted through the lens of Peter's decades of firsthand experience in leading in the public sector.

Acknowledgments

Many people contributed to this book. Foremost were the leaders who generously shared their insights in our interviews: Mollie Anderson, David Bley, Aletha Brown, Cassandra Chandler, Chuck Clarke, Sandy Coleman, Lloyd Douglas, Dick Gregg, Richard Hardos, Robert Keegan, David Lebryk, Sandy MacAdoff, Mary Selecky, Tim Vigotsky, Larry Felix, Diana Gale, Janet White, Judy Brockert, David Skalon, Richard O'Connor, and Jill Vierbuchen. Their accounts of how they approached the various challenges they faced as leaders are fascinating and instructive, and stand in tribute to the capability and commitment of today's leaders in government.

From Peter: The encouragement for and contributions to this work from my family—Carla, Jill, and Meg—just add to the already lengthy list of reasons why I love and appreciate them. Next, I must express my deep appreciation to the many outstanding professionals with whom I worked and from whom I learned so much during my years in government. Unfortunately, there are way too many of them to list here without the risk of inadvertently omitting someone, so as you read this I think you will know who you are—your friendship remains one of the most treasured aspects of my career. Then, I must say, sadly, posthumous thanks to Jim Conlon, my own mentor, who at important times in my career offered much valued personal encouragement and advice and set a high bar for fairness in dealings with all people. I hope I did him proud when I was fortunate enough to later occupy the same leadership position in which he served so well. Finally, in a class by themselves are Michael Watkins and Cate Reavis. Michael, who invited me to work with him on this book, is a long-time friend whose abilities and insights have never ceased to amaze, and whose friendship and understanding have never ceased to be deeply appreciated. Cate's excellence in interviewing the outstanding public-sector executives who contributed to our research provided Michael and me with invaluable insights to the contemporary world of government. Further, her editorial suggestions and challenging questions rescued me from confusion more times than I can count.

From Michael: For me, this book had its deepest roots in my experience of growing up watching my father William Watkins grapple with the joys and sorrows of working in public-sector organizations. I will always be grateful for his wisdom and his love. I was fortunate to be on the faculty of the Kennedy School of Government between 1991 and 1996 and to learn about the public sector from the many talented people there, especially Graham Alison, Merilee Grindle, Ron Heifetz, Linda Kaboolian, Steve Kelman, Marty Linsky, Brian Mandell, Mark Moore, John Thomas, and Mick Trainor, as well as the dedicated staff of KSG executive programs. It also was during this period that I met Peter Daly. I feel very fortunate to have gotten to know Pete and to have benefited from his very deep experience of serving the public interest. My heartfelt thanks too to Cate for all her efforts in bringing this project to fruition. I also have benefited and continue to benefit greatly from conversations with participants in the National Security programs run by KSG, both military and civilian. Finally, thanks to my wife Shawna and my children, Aidan, Maeve, and Niall, who put up with me during the book-writing process.

The
First
90
Days
in Government

Introduction:
Getting Up to Speed

To STRIVE AND FAIL to be chosen for a leadership role is painful; to strive and succeed can be downright intimidating. Why? Because taking a new role means leaving behind the confines of what you know how to do well and embarking on an often uncomfortable journey of personal development. It means moving from a position where you understood the politics and had formed key alliances to one where all this connective tissue has to be rebuilt. It means redefining for yourself, and for others, the roles you play in organizations. For the leaders we interviewed, transitions were exhilarating but they were also, and for good reason, sources of considerable anxiety, especially in the first few critical months of taking charge in a new role.

If you are reading this, you most likely have recently been selected to take a new leadership role in a governmental agency. Or perhaps you aspire to leadership and are considering in what areas you need development. In any case, your new role will involve promotion to a position that may put you in charge of your former peers. Or it may mean moving from a specialized role to a general manager position responsible for overseeing several different functions. Often, a promotion means leaving one agency and moving to another, confronting you with the need to adapt to an entirely new culture and to acquire new knowledge and build new relationships to get things done. And, especially at the senior executive levels, you may be caught up in the postelection changing of the guard, which will require you to establish working relationships with a new set of political appointees and, perhaps, to undertake different sorts of policy initiatives. So, while you probably are excited about being selected for your new position, you rightly may be apprehensive about how you will meet the challenges that lie ahead.

You are not alone. Each year more than two hundred fifty thousand public-sector managers in the United States alone transition to new, usually higher-level, jobs.[1] Others enter the public sector following careers in for-profit or nonprofit management. Regardless, these managers are all confronted with new demands to learn; establish relationships with bosses, subordinates, and key stakeholders; develop a vision for the new organization; enact that vision; and evaluate their own performance as well as that of others.

Confronting the Transition Challenge

Transitions are times of opportunity and vulnerability. For every successful transition by a leader in government, there are many examples of talented leaders with sterling records of performance who stumbled along the way, damaging their careers and the organizations they were charged to help lead. You're reading this book because you don't want to be one of them.

Why is your transition period so important? For one thing, the people who selected you did so because they expect you to add value—and the quicker they see that you are doing so, the better it will be for you and your agency. For another, your new organization will be watching and waiting for you to establish a tempo. Key members of your new team will take their cues about the urgency and importance of their own contributions from you.

Getting off to a slow or disorganized start or falling into one of the classic leadership traps early on can seriously undermine your ability to succeed. Make a few mistakes and you will feel as if you are pushing a boulder uphill from that point onward, potentially causing you to fail to meet your and your agency's performance expectations.

Failure brings both personal and social costs. New leaders who fall into transition traps will, in some cases, be dismissed. More usually, they will find themselves exiled to a bureaucratic Siberia. In contrast to the business world, government programs usually have a much higher public profile, a greater number of stakeholders, and a wider range of influence, so performance failures by government can have consequences measured not just by financial standards but also by public embarrassment, political defeats, and in some cases even by life or death.

How do you avoid these pitfalls? By quickly getting up to speed with the challenges and vulnerabilities you face. Consider the story of two hikers who encounter a tiger in the jungles of Sumatra.[2] One hiker turns to the other and says, "There's no point in running. That tiger is faster than we are." "I disagree," replies the other. "The question is not whether the tiger is faster than us, but whether I'm faster than you."

Although conditions within government organizations are not quite so treacherous as those faced by our hikers, two essential lessons for new leaders emerge from this parable. The first is that when you find yourself in a new and unfamiliar situation, it is essential that you quickly grasp the risks and opportunities and adjust your strategy accordingly. From observing new leaders in government and discussing their experiences (the good and not so good) upon entering their new leadership roles, we've learned that failure is rarely just about the flaws of individuals—after all, most new leaders are quite talented and have had significant successes in the past. Nor is failure usually about being caught in no-win situations where success is not realistically attainable. Most failures are the result of mismatches between the situation, with its challenges and opportunities, and the individual, with his or her strengths and weaknesses.

The second lesson is that knowing the right questions to ask can make the difference between success and failure. Meeting the particular challenges confronting new public-sector managers in the face of scarce resources, rising demand for services, and often contentious political environments requires asking yourself such key questions as: What am I expected to accomplish? What must I learn? How can I gain influence over events that will affect my success? How will I design my strategy? How will I manage my personal life and balance the new stresses I will be experiencing? If you fail to pose and answer these questions, you shouldn't be surprised if you end up as tiger bait.

Transitioning in the Public Sector

Although much good work has been done on leadership in the public sector, surprisingly little of it addresses one of the most pressing problems facing any new government manager: accelerating your own transition into a challenging new role. Most writing on this topic is addressed to executives in the business world, and, accordingly, the strategies for success tend to be formulated in the context of business realities and corporate culture.

This book is written specifically for the professional government manager (though there is much in it that political appointees and even legislators would find useful). It is grounded in the belief that, though there are some similarities, there are critical differences between the private sector and public sector that go to the heart of how success and failure are defined, measured, and either rewarded or penalized.

What makes public-sector transitions so different? Roy Ash, past chairman and CEO of Litton Industries and one-time director of the Office of Management and Budget, once observed that leadership in business and government are alike only in their least important aspects. Going from business to government, he said, is like going from the minor to the major leagues in professional sports.[3]

There is much truth in Ash's observation. All sports have rule books, but in public-sector leadership, the book is thicker and its relevance to what is happening on the playing field is not always as clear as it is in the private sector. All sports have spectators, but the observers of government action are often noisier and more contentious than those who observe and interpret the competitive battles between firms in the marketplace. And, finally, it's much more difficult to figure out "the score" in government than it is in business. Results often are ambiguous and take time to emerge; one often is left wondering whether the outcome was a win or a loss.

Much of what makes the public and private sectors different stems from how they define success. One of the executives interviewed for this book pointed to the unique challenges facing public-sector mangers, stating: "There is no board of directors to provide specific direction on what is to be done. You need to be a self-starter if you're going to be successful because there's nobody to lay it out for you."

In particular, public-sector leaders face the following challenges:

- The mission, goals, and metrics of performance often are dictated by rigid statute or regulation beyond the control of the executive or those to whom he or she reports.

- Performance is subject to a high degree of transparency and often shifting, impatient public scrutiny.

- The stakeholders who exert influence over organizational performance are not only much vaster in number than those usually found in the business world, but they also bring to bear a more highly diverse and competitive set of interests.

- Direct access to critical resources often is impeded by opaque, remote, and onerous bureaucratic systems with long lead times.

For newly appointed managers in government, transitions can therefore be daunting due to the constraints placed on independent action and the complexity of the managerial environment common to governments at all levels. Some have described the feeling as akin to being Gulliver, tied down by innumerable tiny strings. Others have described it as managing with one hand tied behind your back. But no matter what the conditions, if you are to succeed you must begin with an achievement-oriented strategy right from the moment you know you will be transitioning to a new leadership role. The point of departure is an appreciation of the new challenges to be faced.

Leading Change

It is inherently more difficult to lead change in public organizations than it is in business. Private-sector organizations, responding to the demands of a dynamic global economy, are far more flexibly structured than their counterparts of just a couple of decades ago. The expectation that change will occur, therefore, makes it relatively straightforward to lead change in the business context.

Public-sector organizations, by contrast, tend to be explicitly designed to promote stability and predictability. The bureaucratic model at the foundation of most government organizations has its roots in the European and American social reforms of the late nineteenth and early twentieth centuries. These reforms sought to replace monarchist or patronage systems of government with ones where people were selected because of expertise and operated under sets of rules rather than at the whim of autocrats. The organizations that resulted were:

- Governed by a complicated written set of formal relationships into which entry is controlled by rigidly defined sets of qualifications.

- Staffed by people specializing in narrowly defined tasks that are strictly prescribed by rules (and less by cultural norms), and where power is distributed in a clear hierarchy.

- Overseen by professional managers who have the principal responsibility to assure that everything is done according to the rules, and where decisions are made on rational considerations of the organization's best interests rather than on the personal feelings of individuals.

While compliance with each of these characteristics has been notoriously uneven over the century or so that American government has been so organized, the bureaucratic model, with its core bias for stability, still dominates the public-sector landscape. The upshot? It is bound to be very challenging to lead change in public-sector organizations; your counterparts in business have a much easier time of it.

But success is by no means impossible. There are many inspiring examples of forward-looking and talented leaders crafting well-managed, creative, and effective government programs at the federal, state, and local levels, including:

- In Baltimore, a mayoral initiative called Citistat has greatly improved responsiveness to citizens' calls for services, ranging from building permits, to property tax issues, to water and sewage matters, to pet licenses—and everything in between.

- In the City of Seattle, creative environmental planning has resulted in the substitution of plants and trees for the traditional pipes in directing and purifying runoff water that flows into lakes and streams.

- At the federal level, the Department of Health and Human Services pioneered an online source for critically ill patients to obtain vital information related to clinical trials.

These winners of the Innovations in American Government Award, presented by the Ford Foundation and Harvard's Kennedy School of Government, are but a few of the many truly excellent government programs designed by public-sector leaders to address a significant problem and efficiently deliver tangible results to the American people.

Adopting a Systematic Approach

To surmount the challenges of public-sector transitions, avoid the traps that lead to failure, and achieve needed change, you must engage in careful, systematic planning. Why should you use a structured process for planning your transition to a new leadership role? After all, isn't "paralysis by analysis" a part of what makes it so hard to lead change in government? And aren't there plenty of examples of highly successful charismatic leaders who worked on instinct alone and left the details to others?

The answer is "rarely." Leaders who do successfully rely on instinct rather than planning usually are found in nascent political or religious movements or in entrepreneurial start-ups. Even for them, once the initial success of their leadership in building the enterprise is achieved, control of its future usually is transferred to professional managers for whom careful planning is the key to longer-term success. These leaders are rarely, if ever, found directly leading key operations within the kind of complex operating environments found in most government agencies.

Most of the high-achieving government managers we interviewed had at one time or another taken on new leadership positions in organizations that were in crisis. They were eloquent about the dangers of making high-stakes transitions without careful planning, likening it to flying an airplane blind in a storm. Everything *might* turn out OK, but the potential to crash into an unseen hillside is great, and the consequences—to your organization and to you personally—are too potentially devastating to risk operating on instinct and experience alone.

Reaching the Breakeven Point

Our goal is to provide a blueprint for dramatically condensing the time it will take you to get on top of your new job. The length of transition periods varies more widely in government than in business, but your goal should still be to get up to speed as quickly as possible. Put another way, you should strive to arrive as rapidly as possible at the *breakeven point,* where you are a net contributor of value to your new organization. Every minute you save by being systematic about accelerating your transition is a minute you gain to create value in your new role.

The breakeven point is the point at which new leaders have contributed as much value to their new organization as they have consumed from it. As shown in figure I-1, new leaders are net consumers

FIGURE I-1

The breakeven point

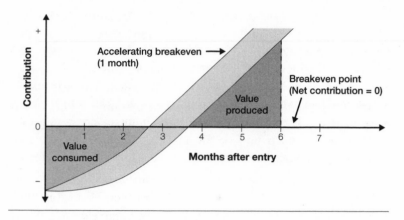

of value early on; as they learn and begin to take action, they begin to create value. From the breakeven point onward, they are (one hopes) net contributors of value to their organizations. The purpose of transition acceleration, then, is to help new leaders reach the breakeven point earlier.

Research on leadership transitions in business indicates it takes about six months before a mid-senior-level manager reaches this point.[4] But in government we have found that the length of successful transition periods varies widely. In some cases, demands for results may be more immediate due to past agency performance failures, political exigency, public-policy imperatives, or high public scrutiny. In others, more time is available for the new manager to acquire the knowledge needed to reach the breakeven point. Regardless, what you do upon entering your new job will have a disproportionate effect on your later success. That is why the first months of transition to a new assignment are so important, and why transition planning is so critical. There are, again, important differences between the corporate world and government in the way value is measured.

In corporations, the case for accelerated and better quality transitions rests on cost avoidance; the quicker a new leader reaches the breakeven point and begins to contribute positively to the business, the quicker the company begins to realize a return on its investment in his or her recruitment and initial salary payout. In government, however, political embarrassment tends to trump cost, and the case for accelerated transitions at the seniormost levels rests on shortening the period during which mistakes are likely to be made. These mistakes can be picked up in the media, play into the positions of political opponents, erode credibility, or create a public uproar—all of which impede an administration's governance efforts. Cost avoidance plays a somewhat more important role deeper within an agency, though, where reducing the time it takes for a new manager to get on top of his or her new job can have a direct effect on budgets and agencywide plans for efficiency or financial performance improvements.

Following the Transition Road Map

Leadership is ultimately about leverage. Effective leaders leverage themselves—their ideas, energy, relationships, and influence—to create new patterns in organizations. The leader is just one person, and usually one person can accomplish very little alone. The ability to leverage yourself rests in turn on perceptions of personal credibility and demonstrated effectiveness. Small initial successes yield leadership capital that can be invested to yield even larger returns. The underlying goal of the strategies presented in this book—whether those strategies are defining objectives, creating alliances, or building a team—is to help new leaders in government build momentum and thus increase their leverage.

The rest of the book provides a road map for accelerating your transition. The conceptual backbone of the road map is captured in nine key transition challenges:

1. **Clarify expectations.** Because no other single relationship is more important, you need to figure out how to build a

productive working relationship with your new boss and understand his or her expectations. You also need to understand and factor in the expectations of other key stakeholders. Clarifying expectations means carefully planning for a series of critical conversations about the situation, expectations, style, resources, and your personal development.

2. **Match strategy to situation.** Though there are certain overarching principles that apply to all transitions, there are no hard-and-fast rules for achieving success in every transition situation. Instead, you need to diagnose the situation accurately and determine its challenges and opportunities. Starting up an agency or unit, for example, entails challenges that are different from those you'd face while turning around an organization in serious trouble. A clear diagnosis of the situation is an essential prerequisite for developing your action plan.

3. **Accelerate your learning.** You need to climb the learning curve as fast as you can in your new organization. This means understanding the organization's mission, services, technologies, systems, and structures, as well as its culture and politics. Getting acquainted with a new organization can feel like drinking from a fire hose. You have to be systematic and focused about deciding what you need to learn and how you will learn it most efficiently.

4. **Secure early wins.** You need to translate expectations and your diagnosis of the situation into a set of goals—results to be achieved and behaviors to be changed—that you will accomplish by the end of your first year. In parallel with this you need to figure out where and how you will get early wins to build your credibility, create momentum, and lay the foundation for achieving your longer-term goals.

5. **Build the team.** If you are inheriting a team, as is the case in most government transition situations, you will need to evaluate its members and perhaps restructure it to better meet

the demands of the situation. Your willingness to make tough calls and your ability to select the right people for the right positions are among the most important skills you will call on during your transition. You will need to be both systematic and strategic in approaching the team-building challenge.

6. **Create alliances.** Your success will depend on your ability to influence people outside your direct line of control. Supportive alliances, both internal and external, will be necessary to achieve your goals. You should, therefore, start right away to identify whose support is essential for your success and to determine how to line those people up on your side.

7. **Achieve alignment.** The higher you rise in an organization, the more you have to play the role of organizational architect. This means figuring out whether the organization's strategy is sound, bringing its structure into alignment with its strategy, and developing the systems and skill bases necessary to realize strategic intent.

8. **Avoid predictable surprises.** All too often new leaders get off to a good start only to have something blow up and take them off track. While true surprises happen, many so-called surprises are in fact foreseeable and avoidable. To avoid what we call "predictable surprises," you need to understand the most common reasons why they happen and take early actions to identify potential threats.

9. **Manage yourself.** In the personal and professional tumult of a transition, you will have to work hard to maintain your equilibrium and preserve your ability to make good judgments. The risks of losing perspective, getting isolated, and making bad calls are ever present during transitions. There is much you can do to accelerate your personal transition and to gain more control over your work environment. The right advice-and-counsel network is an indispensable resource.

If you succeed in meeting these core challenges, you will have a successful transition. Failure to surmount any one of them, however, is enough to cause potentially crippling problems. The chapters that follow offer actionable guidelines and tools for succeeding in meeting each of these challenges. You will learn how to diagnose your situation and create action plans tailored to your needs, regardless of your level in the organization or the situation you face.

As illustrated in figure I-2, there is a sequential logic to moving though these chapters. Early on in your transition, the overriding goal is to *diagnose* your situation so that you can develop situation-appropriate strategies. Using this early learning as a foundation, you can *define* the goals you will seek to achieve as you strive to secure some early wins and build a foundation for improvement in your new organization.

FIGURE I-2

The transition road map

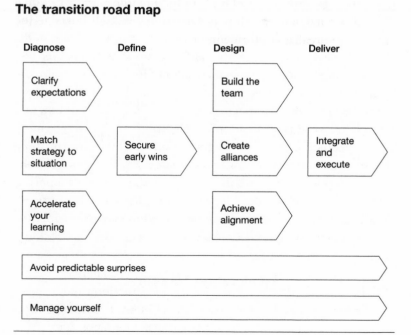

Clarity about situation and goals, in turn, allows you to think through the key *design* questions concerning your team, the alliances you need to build, and the changes you need to make in the organization's architecture. Then, of course, you have to integrate these elements and *deliver* results. Throughout this process you have to keep your eyes open so that you don't get predictably surprised. Critically, you have to manage yourself by identifying potential vulnerabilities and compensating for them.

This is not to say that these are a fixed set of phases through which you will proceed in a linear fashion. In addition, the time you devote to these activities will vary widely depending on the particular situation you face. At the same time, the road map will help you build a robust transition plan.

The transition road map can be applied in all public organizations. Bureaucracies of every kind depend on a clear chain of command to carry out the mission, so, though there are differences in perspective between agency heads, program leaders, and functional managers, each of these levels of leadership is directly linked to the agency's ultimate goals through a carefully designed system of defined responsibilities, authority, and accountability. Whether you are assuming leadership of an internal staff function, of a major operating unit, or of the agency itself, the principles of transition remain the same. But the specifics of who, what, when, and how and the relative weights of the nine key challenges vary a lot. For more senior people, aligning the organization's architecture, building the team, and creating alliances loom large. For less senior people, building a relationship with the new boss and creating a supportive advice-and-counsel network will be priorities. Every new leader needs to quickly become familiar with the new organization, to secure early wins, and to build supportive alliances.

Accelerating Everyone

Finally, as you read the book, think about how you can help others in your organization accelerate their transitions. Consider the following: How many people transition into new managerial positions, including leading a task force or special project, in your organization in a typical year? What would you estimate the value of accelerating those transitions by just 5 percent to be?

The quicker you can get new direct reports up to speed, the more you will be able to accelerate your own performance. Beyond that, the benefits to the organization of systematically accelerating everyone's transitions are potentially vast. Leaving people to flounder about in transitions wastes time, energy, and talent. Good organizations use transitions into demanding positions to develop high-potential leadership talent; they don't abandon their most precious resources to sink or swim. If you are able to teach people the transition-acceleration skills they need to maximize their chances for success, you will also be better able to discern whose abilities really stand out.

Conclusion

As you prepare to take on new leadership responsibilities, remember that your transition will be a time of opportunity and risk—a time to demonstrate your ability to capitalize on your strengths and to hedge your weaknesses with astute planning. During this rewarding but often perilous period you must quickly and correctly understand the nature of your new leadership assignment and be aware of the keys to success as well as the potential traps that can lead to failure. Grasping this right at the start is as essential to the achievement of your long-term career goals as it was to the hikers' goal of not becoming tiger food.

That's why this book is not just another collection of theories. Instead, it provides practical guidelines for translating principles into plans tailored to your own situation. As you continue through it, read actively, making notes about the applicability of specific points to your situation, and think about how to apply the advice to your situation.

Clarify Expectations

WHEN KEVIN CODY was appointed management development director in the newly created office of human resources in a major federal department, he believed he knew precisely what he needed to do. The organization had recently experienced a major reorganization and downsizing, and the shockwaves were still echoing. After several years working as a largely self-directed senior training specialist at large departmental field offices, where he enjoyed a reputation as an energetic self-starter who could be counted on to deliver, Kevin believed himself to be well versed in what it took to become a high-performing leader under such circumstances. He also was thoroughly familiar with the government-wide policies that determine managerial and executive qualifications.

Kevin reported to his new position at the department's headquarters in Washington, D.C., just one week after being selected, leaving his wife and two children several hundred miles away to complete the school year before relocating. On his first day he learned that he was entering an organization still in considerable flux. His new boss, the director of human resources, was months away from being officially named to the position. In the interim, Kevin would report to an aide to the assistant secretary for administration, a political appointee who had been in his position about six months. Furthermore, only two of Kevin's four peer positions in the HR office were filled. Finally, he learned that of the twelve positions reporting to him, only three were filled with experienced training professionals; the balance were staffed with transfers resulting from the elimination of other functions during the reorganization.

Because it was budget preparation time, Kevin wasn't able to meet with his interim boss until his second week on the job. The first face-to-face meeting lasted fifteen minutes and consisted of a welcoming handshake and a question or two about Kevin's background and what he planned to do. This informal and ambiguous introduction was quite different from what he had experienced in previous assignments. In the past, his new role as well as his bosses' expectations had been clearly defined from the beginning. Now Kevin found himself in an entirely new environment with distracted leadership and a staff of unknown ability.

Recognizing that his previous experience had not prepared him for this situation, Kevin's self-starter instincts kicked in. He decided to prepare a memo to his interim boss, laying out what he planned to do for the next three months—assess the staff, survey supervisory and management-training needs among the departments' senior executives, and create a departmental management-training plan and budget—and then just go ahead and do it. He figured if there was a problem with what he planned to do, he would hear about it.

As he moved forward, Kevin only occasionally heard from the assistant secretary's aide to whom he was nominally reporting. The conversations were brief and inconsequential, so he believed he was on the right track and forged ahead. At the beginning of his fourth month, Kevin delivered his training plan and budget to the aide, and soon after all hell broke loose.

Kevin's plan called for a fundamental overhaul of the department's training and management-development strategy. He recommended that management-training funds be removed from the individual budgets of program heads and pooled under his control. Moreover, in formulating the plan, Kevin had consulted with supervisory union representatives and incorporated many of their suggestions. When he independently sent his plan around to program heads for comment, it wasn't long before the assistant secretary's phone began ringing. Equally damaging, the staff aide who was supposed to be overseeing Kevin's work, and who had been too distracted with political tasks to thoroughly read Kevin's original memo, was in the hot seat. As a career executive now caught up in an unanticipated maelstrom of political reaction, Kevin saw his fast start come to a screeching halt. Privately, he began planning his return to his previous position.

The number one challenge you will face as a newly appointed public-sector leader like Kevin is clarifying expectations concerning what you will accomplish in your new role. To surmount this challenge, you must engage in a focused effort to figure out what is required of you; to assess the associated risks, constraints, and opportunities; and to actively shape expectations. Critically, this means understanding the agendas of stakeholders and carefully diagnosing the political environment you are about to enter.

Navigating the Expectations Minefield

How did Kevin get himself into so much trouble so quickly with his new bosses? He failed to clarify expectations. Though he understood that his previous experience was not a perfect fit with his new situation, he did not allocate the time for personally learning about the highly politicized environment in which he now found himself. Instead, he fell back on what had worked for him in the past—his strong sense of self-direction—and took off on his own, assuming his distracted superiors would be pleased. He got into trouble not because his work wasn't full of good ideas, but because he failed to recognize the need to have, to force if need be, critical conversations with his bosses early on and to clarify their expectations before undertaking major initiatives.

Kevin's well-intentioned choice to pursue his plan on his own set his bosses up for a rude surprise from their political colleagues. Had he invested more time and persistence in connecting with his new bosses, understanding the situations they were facing and what they expected from him in the way of reporting, the result, while perhaps less efficiently executed, would have been much better for everyone concerned.

To avoid ending up in Kevin's situation, keep in mind that the task of managing expectations commences the moment you learn you are being considered for a new position; for new leaders coming in from outside the agency, this means during the job interviews. But be careful! Because new leaders want to impress and because new bosses sometimes expect miracles, it is all too easy to set unrealistic expectations early on. While the new boss may want to negotiate expectations at the outset of a transition, the new leader usually lacks a sufficiently comprehensive understanding of the situation he or she will face and, thus, will not be able to fully grasp what is and is not realistic.

It's all too easy to fall into the resulting trap of attempting too much too soon. To avoid setting yourself up for failure, it is essential that you engage in regular conversations with your boss to achieve initial agreement on what the problem is, what the solution would look like, and how it might be achieved. At the same time, you should never assume that your initial mandate will or should remain unchanged; you should be prepared to make appropriate adjustments along the way.

Diagnosing the Situation

One common reason for failure among newly appointed government managers is misreading the situations they face in their new leadership position. The result is underestimated risks, off-the-mark performance metrics, wrongly established goals, and inappropriately constructed strategies. Understanding the situation you are entering as a new leader is, therefore, a crucial prerequisite for designing a successful transition strategy.

One tool for assessing your situation is the ST_ARS *model,* an acronym for *s*tart-up, *t*urnaround, *r*ealignment, and *s*ustaining success.[1] The ST_ARS model is a tool for analyzing opportunities and risks in each of four common types of transition situations:

- **Start-up.** The least common situation faced by government managers. Usually precipitated by a new exigency or major policy initiative, this type of challenge demands rapid organizational design and functional integration decisions, under conditions of high public scrutiny. Unsurprisingly, start-up situations tend to be higher risk.

- **Turnaround.** Somewhat more common than start-up situations. Usually precipitated by a major performance failure or a scandal of some kind, these situations involve shake-ups of people and structures under conditions of high public scrutiny. These too are high-risk situations.

- **Realignment.** A fairly typical situation faced by government executives, usually precipitated by shifting political or public-policy imperatives, involving either major reductions or increases in resources, resizing, and retraining under moderate public scrutiny. These tend to be medium-risk situations.

- **Sustaining success.** The most common type of situation faced by government leaders. Usually characterized by a stable mission and established operational structures, these situations may have an expanding or shrinking service base. Major challenges are the defense of existing domain and error avoidance. Though not in any sense risk-free, these tend to be lower-risk situations.

Each of these situations presents a distinct set of transition demands and, therefore, requires different transition strategies for the new leader. In the higher-risk categories of start-up and turnaround, for example, the time available to reach the breakeven point is likely to be considerably shortened by political pressure and public scrutiny. In the medium- to lower-risk categories of realignment and sustaining success, more time may be allowed before results are expected, but effecting change often is more difficult because of entrenched interests and inertia.

Being new to his agency and lacking a full understanding of its strategy and political environment, Kevin Cody's major mistake, driven by his habitual bias for action, was assuming that he faced a turnaround situation, requiring quick and dramatic corrective action, when he actually faced a realignment, requiring just a better matchup between his agency's overall administrative strategy and the extant structure of its management-development programs. Had he taken the time to do a more extensive analysis of the situation he faced, and acquired a clearer understanding of what he was expected to deliver, his self-starter instincts might have been curbed in favor of a more deliberate process of problem diagnosis.

Seeing the Big Picture

A second common mistake is the failure to recognize the full set of stakeholders whose expectations will influence your mandate. Regardless of your level in the organization—first-line supervisor, functional manager, or agency head—it is important for you to develop a working understanding of the broader political, cultural, and regulatory environment within which you operate so that you are better able (1) to comprehend and predict the areas that are likely to be priority concerns in your leadership position, and (2) to tailor your own action plans so that they conform and support those priorities. Understanding the big picture will not only keep you on track with your boss's expectations, but it will also greatly facilitate your ability to anticipate and adjust to shifts in those expectations.

While your direct boss is likely to be the most important person influencing expectations and assessments of your success, he or she is unlikely to be the only one interested in your work. Government organizations almost always have many more stakeholders than businesses do. These stakeholders have widely varying interests and, more often than not, compete with one another.

At the senior levels, external constituencies can create pressures that can easily place professional administrators at odds with their political superiors. If you fail to recognize this and act accordingly, you can easily get caught up in the kind of political maelstrom that engulfed Kevin Cody. If you are deeper within the organization, perhaps a first-line supervisor or middle manager, it's imperative that you understand the conflicting pressures exerted on your boss by those who control key resources, administer various service systems such as personnel and procurement, and audit and evaluate organizational performance. Awareness of these pressures will help you to better plan your activities and to be a more useful—and appreciated—source of internal support for your boss as he or she fights the inevitable bureaucratic battles.

In Kevin's case, he mistakenly approached the task of energizing his agency's management-development activities as though it were an independent effort, unaffected by the wider range of political and financial interests that were very real concerns of his bosses. He was also oblivious to the larger budget issues that were swirling around his agency at the time and devised his proposal for centralized control of training funds on the narrow basis of what would work best for him. If he had insisted on clarifying what was expected of him before launching his proposals, he would have been more aware of the politically competitive environment that exists in formulating budgets and what leverage he did or did not have in that process. Equipped with that knowledge, he then could have framed his proposals so that they fit better with the prevailing interests of such key stakeholders as the political program heads who were competing for the same resources, and who later assailed him to his new bosses.

Engaging Your New Boss

For more than a century, it has been a national governance policy of the United States to foster, at the federal, state, and local levels, a professional civil service charged with the responsibility of executing the policies and programs enacted by elected legislatures and administrations. This policy has given rise to many statutes and regulations meant to insulate the civil service from patronage and other forms of undue political influence.

These constraints have made the relationship between employees and managers in government quite different in many respects from that typically found in the private sector. Nevertheless, just as new managers have major influence on the performance and aspirations of their subordinates, their bosses have influence on them. Although their authority to hire and fire, discipline, and reward is limited by employee protections, the need to negotiate success with the boss remains a primary requirement for new managers at every level.

Your relationship with your new boss will be built through continuing dialogue. Ideally, your discussions will begin before you accept the new position and continue into your transition and beyond. But in many situations in government you will not be able to adequately talk with your new boss before the transition begins. When this happens, it is imperative that you move quickly to make up for lost time by engaging with your boss in an energetic and systematic manner.

To structure the dialogue that should take place after you report for your new position, you should focus on five conversations. They are not necessarily subjects to be dealt with separately, or in single meetings. Rather, they are intertwined themes to discuss whenever appropriate.

The Situation Conversation

Your goal with the situation conversation is to gain an understanding of how your new boss sees the state of your new organization. Is it a turnaround, a start-up, a realignment, or a sustaining-success situation? How did the organization reach this point, and what factors make this situation a challenge? What resources within the larger organization can you draw on? Once you learn more, your perceptions may differ from your boss's, but understanding how he or she sees the situation is essential if you are later to achieve a *shared* understanding of what challenges and opportunities lie ahead. This information will be the foundation for what you do next. Kevin Cody was never able to learn how his bosses accessed his situation, and this failure led to a lot of serious problems.

The Expectations Conversation

Your agenda with the expectations conversation will be to clarify and negotiate what you are expected to accomplish. What is expected of you in the short term and the medium term? What will constitute success? How and when will your performance be measured? You might conclude that your boss's expectations are unrealistic and that you need to work to reset them. So keep in mind the basic principle that it is better to underpromise and overdeliver than overpromise and underdeliver. At the same time, you must work to actively shape expectations. Remember, if you do not manage them, they will manage you.

The Style Conversation

The style conversation is about how you and your boss can best interact on an ongoing basis. What is his or her preferred form of communication—face-to-face, e-mail, voice mail, memos? How often are status reports expected? What sorts of decisions does he or she want to be consulted on, and when are you expected to make the call on your own? Keep in mind that your boss will have a comfort zone about his or her involvement in decision making. Think of this zone as defining the boundaries of the decision-making "box" in which you will operate. Initially, expect to be confined to a relatively small box. As your new boss gains confidence in you, the box should grow larger. If it doesn't, or if it remains too small to allow you to be effective, you may have to address the issue directly. Failure to gain clarity on these issues was at the heart of the troubles that Kevin got himself into.

The Resources Conversation

The resources conversation is actually a negotiation for critical resources. What do you need to be successful? These resources are not limited to people and funds (in many government contexts, some of these may be beyond the power of your boss to provide).

You might also need support from your boss and more senior managers when it comes to implementing change. In a start-up situation, your most urgent needs are likely to be adequate financial resources, technical support, and people with the right expertise. In a turnaround situation, you need authority, backed by political support, to make the tough decisions and secure scarce financial and human resources. In a realignment situation, you need consistent, public backing to get the organization to confront the need for change. Ideally, your boss will stand shoulder to shoulder with you, helping pierce through denial and complacency. In a sustaining-success situation, you will require financial and technical resources to sustain the core of what the agency does well. Some suggestions for negotiating for resources are presented in "Negotiating for Resources."

Negotiating for Resources

As you seek commitments for resources, keep these principles of effective negotiation in mind:

- *Focus on underlying interests.* Probe as deeply as possible to understand the agendas of your boss and any others to whom you will need to apply for resources. What is in it for them?

- *Look for mutually beneficial exchanges.* Seek resources that both support your boss's agenda and advance your own. Look for ways to help peers advance their agendas in return for help with yours.

- *Link resources to results.* Highlight the performance benefits that will result if more resources are dedicated to your unit. Create a "menu" laying out what you can achieve (and not achieve) with current resources and what different sized increments would allow you to do.

The Personal Development Conversation

The personal development conversation is a discussion of how your tenure and performance in this job can contribute to your own growth. In what areas do you need strengthening? Are there special projects you could undertake that will help your development without taking away from your primary focus? Are there formal training courses available that would improve your capabilities?

Putting It All Together

In practice, your dialogue about these subjects may be intermingled with other topics and evolve over time. You might address several of the five issues in a single meeting, or you might work out issues related to one subject through a series of brief exchanges. There is logic to the sequence just described, however. Your earliest conversations should focus on situational diagnosis, expectations, and style. As you learn more, you will be better prepared to negotiate for resources, revisiting your diagnosis of the situation and resetting expectations as needed. When you feel the relationship is reasonably well established, you can introduce the personal development issue. Take some time to plan to discuss each of these subjects, and clearly signal to your boss what you hope to accomplish in each exchange.

Of course, in government structures the way you discuss these issues will differ when the exchange is between very senior career executives and political appointees, versus between middle managers and program directors. At the higher levels, resource and style discussions are likely to be more consuming than, say, personal development issues. As the discussions move down through the organizational hierarchy, however, all five issues come into prominent play.

The situation in which Kevin Cody found himself will be easily recognizable to many government managers. If he had been diligent and patient in having these conversations, the risk of his taking off in the wrong direction would have been substantially reduced.

Do's and Don'ts

When managers were queried about their transition experiences, and how they went about establishing a productive relationship with their new bosses, some key similarities emerged. These are summarized below in the form of some do's and don'ts. Following are some of the don'ts to keep in mind:

- **Don't trash the past.** There is nothing to be gained by criticizing your predecessors. You need to understand what went on before you arrived on the scene, but concentrate on assessing the current situation and on making changes to improve performance. Besides, some of the people responsible may still be in positions of power and influence.

- **Don't stay away.** If you, like Kevin Cody, have a boss who doesn't reach out to you or with whom you have uncomfortable initial encounters, you will have to reach out yourself. Otherwise, you allow potentially dangerous communication gaps to form that can lead to your heading off in the wrong direction. It may feel good to have a lot of rope at first, but you must resist the urge to take it. Get on your boss's calendar regularly, and be sure that he or she is aware of the issues you are facing and that you are aware of his or her expectations and how they may be shifting.

- **Don't surprise your boss.** It is no fun bringing your new boss bad news. Most bosses consider it a far greater problem, however, when subordinates fail to report emerging problems early enough. The worst case is when your boss learns of a problem from another source, say the White House or the governor's mansion, the legislature, the media, or his or her own direct bosses. So it is usually best to give your boss a heads-up as soon as you become aware of a developing problem.

- **Don't approach your boss only with problems.** You don't want to become known as someone who dumps problems on your boss for him or her to solve; you should have a plan ready too. The plan need not be a full-blown description of a solution, but you should always brainstorm a few ways of addressing the problem you are reporting before presenting it to your boss.

- **Don't run down a checklist.** There is a tendency to use meetings with your boss as an opportunity to run down a list of specific accomplishments that, for one reason or another, you feel are important. This is not necessarily what your boss wants to hear on a regular basis; usually he or she will assume you are busy and will expect you to come in only when there is a problem you need help with. There are times, such as formal progress reviews, when going through a list of accomplishments is appropriate, but on most occasions when you and your boss meet, a short presentation of what you are trying to do and how he or she might help will suffice.

- **Don't try to change your boss.** One successful manager told a story about scheduling a midafternoon meeting with his boss and immediately launching into a review of an important issue only to discover that the boss was falling asleep. It turned out that the boss's need for an afternoon nap was well known around the organization, and midafternoon meeting times were avoided. The point is that you cannot change your boss's style, so learn to adapt to it.

You can also follow some fundamental do's to make life with your new boss easier:

- **Do take full responsibility for making the relationship work.** This is the flip side of "Don't stay away." Don't assume that your boss will make an effort to reach out to you or to offer the support that you need. It is best to take responsibility yourself for figuring out how to make the relationship work, and you can be surprised if your boss decides to meet you halfway.

- **Do clarify mutual expectations early and often.** Avoid the fundamental mistake Kevin Cody made and begin managing expectations right away. You too will find yourself in serious trouble if the boss expects you to get something done fast when you know that there are major obstacles to accomplishing it, or if he or she expects you to clear things first only to hear from others that you have gone out on your own. When you have bad news to report, it is wise to get it on the table early and to work to lower unreasonable expectations. This often is not an easy task because many bosses, especially those in politically appointed positions with short time horizons, just don't like to be told no and may tend to raise doubts about your leadership skills when you approach them about adjusting a project schedule or a program implementation deadline. Nevertheless, sometimes reporting bad news is necessary, and one way of lessening the negative fallout is to check in regularly with reports of problems as well as proposals for overcoming them.

- **Do negotiate time lines for diagnosis and action planning.** Don't let yourself get caught up in firefighting or be pressured to make decisions or take actions before you are ready. Buy yourself time to diagnose your situation and come up with a sensible action plan that carries a high chance of success.

- **Do aim for early wins that are important to your boss.** Because of regular changes in political leadership, the priorities of professional government managers often shift dramatically. What was considered highly important to one administration may be an anathema to the next. A critical element in meeting the expectations challenge, therefore, is to clarify what your boss cares about most, and being ready to adjust your own plans accordingly.

- **Do pursue good reviews from those whose opinions your boss respects.** In part, your reputation with the new leadership will be based on what your boss hears about you from trusted sources. You must be aware of who these sources are and how information moves through them. We do not advocate pandering, a sure way to breed distrust in your integrity, but simply a realistic assessment of the influential parties of whom you should be aware.

Dealing with Specific Challenges

As you learn more about your situation, you may find that you are dealing with one or more of the following specific challenges in dealing with your new boss.

Parts of the Organization Are Untouchable

If there are parts of the organization—services, facilities, people—about which your new boss is proprietary, it is essential to figure out what they are as soon as possible. You don't want to find out that you are pressing to reduce funding for the program that your boss started up or to replace someone who has been his or her loyal ally. So try to deduce what your boss is sensitive about. You can do this by understanding his or her personal history, by talking to others, and by paying close attention to facial expression, tone, and body language. If you are uncertain, float an idea gently as a trial balloon, and then watch your boss's reactions closely.

Your Boss's Expectations Are Unrealistic

You may find your boss's expectations unrealistic, or simply at odds with your own beliefs about what needs to be done. If so, you will have to work hard to make your views converge with your boss's. In a realignment situation, for example, your boss may attribute the worst problems to a certain part of the organization, whereas you believe they lie elsewhere. In this case, you will need to educate your boss about the underlying problems to reset expectations. Proceed carefully—especially if your boss feels invested in the way things have always been done or is partially responsible for the problems.

Your Boss's Expectations Are Unclear or Shifting

Even if you are sure you know what your boss expects, you should go back regularly to confirm and clarify. Some bosses know what they want but are not good at expressing it; you could reach clarity only after you have headed down the wrong road. So you have to be prepared to keep asking questions until you are sure you understand. Try, for example, asking the same questions in different ways to gain more insight. Work at reading between the lines accurately and developing good hypotheses about what your boss is likely to want. Try to put yourself in your boss's shoes and understand how he or she will be evaluated. Figure out how you fit into the larger picture. Above all, don't let key issues remain unclear. Ambiguity about goals and expectations is dangerous. As one new leader explained a conflict over what was said about expectations in an earlier conversation, "A tie doesn't go to you; it goes to your supervisor."

You Have Multiple Bosses

You face even more daunting challenges in managing expectations if you have more than one boss. The same fundamental principles hold, but the relative emphasis shifts. If you have multiple bosses, you have to be sure to balance perceived wins and losses among them carefully. If one boss has substantially more power, then it makes sense to bias yourself somewhat in his or her direction early on, so long as you achieve balance to the greatest extent possible later. If you can't get agreement by working with your bosses one-on-one, you have to essentially force them to come to the table together to thrash issues out.

You Have a Virtual Boss

Managing when you are located far from your boss presents a different set of challenges. The risk of falling out of step without realizing it is naturally greater. The distance between you and your boss puts the onus on you to exert even more discipline over communication, scheduling calls and meetings to be sure that you stay aligned. It also is even more critical to establish clear and comprehensive metrics so that your boss gets a reasonable picture of what is going on and you can manage effectively by exception.

There Are Conflicts Between Policy and the Mission

Situations when policy and the mission are at odds are common in some government agencies, where existing statutes or regulations assign responsibilities that might come in conflict with a new administration's policy preferences. The range of these conflicts can involve such macro-level issues as how aggressively the agency carries out its assigned mission to such micro-level matters as the administration of agency-specific affirmative action programs. In these cases, senior-level leaders must proceed carefully, relying on legal counsel and oversight authorities to reconcile the differences. Precarious political positioning often goes with the job of senior career executives, but it is an area fraught with risk and one that must be judiciously handled, particularly with new bosses, so that you can avoid being immediately labeled as an obstructionist or, worse, an ally of the political opposition.

Creating a Transition Plan

No matter what type of situation you are entering, it can be useful to put together a transition plan and to get buy-in from your boss and, if appropriate, other key constituencies. Usually, you will be able to devise a plan after a few weeks in the new role, when you have begun to connect with the organization and get the lay of the land.

Your transition plan should be captured in writing, even if it just consists of bullet points. It should specify priorities and goals as well as milestones. Critically, you should share your plan with your boss and seek buy-in for it. It should serve as a contract between the two of you about how you are going to spend your time, spelling out both what you will do and what you will not do.

To begin to develop your plan, think of your transition as consisting of the four major phases of activity outlined in the transition road map presented in the introduction:

- Diagnosing the situation

- Defining goals

- Designing the foundation for success

- Delivering results

You should typically devote the first block of time to diagnosis: learning and clarifying expectations. Your key outputs at the end of this phase will be a diagnosis of the situation, identification of key priorities, and a plan for how you will spend your time in the next block. This is the phase during which you will focus on having the situation, style, and expectations conversations with your new boss.

In the second phase, "define," you should establish and clarify your longer-term goals—both for achieving performance improvement and for changing behavior. You also should address where and how you will begin to seek some early wins, actions that build your credibility and create momentum. During this phase you should continue the situation and expectations conversations with your boss and begin to talk about resources.

Depending on the situation and your level in the organization, the third phase, "design," might focus on identifying major initiatives and negotiating the resources necessary to pursue them, as well as fleshing out your initial assessments of strategy and structure and presenting a plan for restructuring your team.

Finally, with your plans in place, you can focus on delivering results and adapting to the inevitable surprises.

The appropriate length of time to devote to each phase will vary widely depending on the situation you face. But it is nonetheless critical that you discipline yourself to plan in this way. Otherwise, time will tend to slip by. At the end of each phase, you should schedule a review meeting with your boss. (Naturally, you will likely interact more often than that.)

Working with Your Subordinates

Finally, you won't merely *have* a new boss; you are likely to *be* a new boss as well. You will almost certainly have new subordinates. Just as you need to develop a productive relationship with your new boss, they too need to work effectively with you. In the past, have you done a good job of helping subordinates succeed in their own transitions? What might you do differently this time?

Think about how to apply all the advice in this chapter to working with your own direct reports. The golden rule of transitions is to transition others as you would wish to be transitioned yourself. The five-conversation framework can help build productive relationships with the people who report to you. Introduce the framework to them right away, and schedule a first conversation with each of them to talk about the situation and your expectations. Get them to do some work before the meeting. See how fast you can accelerate their transitions.

Conclusion

It seems like simple advice, but clarifying what is expected of you in your new leadership position is not always a simple matter. Organizations that are in a confusing state of dysfunction, bosses who are not approachable or who are distracted by other matters, staff members who are inept, disgruntled, or obsequious—all these elements often combine to make it difficult to get an exact early reading on what you are supposed to accomplish and how. Nevertheless, the responsibility falls on you to get it done because failure to do so, and substituting your own often uninformed opinions about what is needed, can lead you right into the situation in which Kevin Cody found himself. Following the steps outlined in this chapter will assist you greatly in planning and executing the establishment of a mandate for your performance in your new position. Without one, you, like Kevin, might make some serious missteps and soon find yourself on the outside looking in.

ACCELERATION CHECKLIST

1. How effectively have you built relationships with new bosses in the past? What have you done well? In what areas do you need improvement?

2. Create a plan for the situation conversation. Based on what you know now, what issues will you raise with your boss in this conversation? What do you want to say up front? In what order do you want to raise issues?

3. Create a plan for the expectations conversation. How will you determine what your new boss expects you to do? What about other key constituencies?

4. Create a plan for the style conversation. How will you figure out how your boss prefers to interact with you? What mode of communication (e-mail, voice mail, face-to-face) does he or she prefer? How often should you interact? How much detail should you provide? What types of issues should you consult with him or her about before deciding?

5. Create a plan for the resources conversation. Given what you need to do, what resources are absolutely necessary? If you had fewer resources, what would you have to forgo? If you had more, what would the benefits be?

6. Create a plan for the personal development conversation. What are your strengths, and where do you need improvement? What kinds of assignments or projects might help you develop skills you need?

Match Strategy
to Situation

A S THE FIRST occupant of the newly created position of national director of administrative services at a federal department, Amy Donovan was charged with improving the performance of three quasi-independent regional administrative support centers. Although the centers' performance had raised serious concerns in recent years, each was still providing a host of important staff services to department operations scattered across the country.

A human resource manager with ten years' experience, Amy had only a cursory knowledge of procurement, financial services, real estate, and other areas of support that the centers were tasked with providing. But she did understand that success in building cohesive, high-performing organizations from three that were in varying degrees of trouble would involve much more than simply mastering the details of their work. The number one challenge was to diagnose and consolidate the centers' widely disparate cultures and management styles into a unified approach that promoted efficiency and delivered a high level of customer service across the board.

Amy initiated her diagnostic process by holding an intensive series of review meetings with the directors of the three centers. These managers had been in their positions for years, and Amy rapidly reached the conclusion that they believed they were impervious to change. In truth, they had little reason to embrace new ways of managing as they had ironclad job security. Their near-term removal was simply not an option for Amy due to their seniority, civil service protections, and the disruption that immediate personnel changes might have on the ongoing delivery of the centers' services. The meetings ended with Amy both better informed and wiser not only about the complexity of the situation she faced but also about the resistance she likely would encounter in reforming the organization.

She then traveled to each center to hold meetings with first-line supervisors and working-level employees to learn about their responsibilities and how they carried those responsibilities out, to assess how the centers used resources and technology, and to get a firsthand sense of the different work cultures that existed among the centers. What she discovered were three quite different situations. The first center she visited, led by the director with the shortest tenure, gave her cause for both encouragement and concern. According to her review of past performance records, the center was consistently providing responsive and technically solid support services to its field-office customers. Furthermore, her interviews with supervisors and working-level employees revealed a well-trained and serious-minded workforce proud of their reputation for high performance. She was somewhat troubled, however, by a subtle but detectable attitude of complacency among most center employees. They were so certain of their capability that they did not indicate any areas where improvement was needed. Amy considered this attitude a red flag that trouble could lie ahead.

The second center on her agenda was led by the longest-serving of the three directors. It also was the largest center, serving heavily populated regions of the country. Amy's review of its records revealed a history of high performance that had slipped significantly over the past few years. When she interviewed the supervisory and working-level staff, Amy was taken aback by the smugness she found. The staff simply dismissed the mounting complaints of its customers as "the usual griping" of people who were too demanding and who did not understand the difficulty of providing the level of service they seemed to think they were due. When asked how often staffers met or communicated with their customer offices, Amy was told by the center director that he believed it was not their role to do that. Rather, he felt it was their job to evaluate whatever complaints came up and decide whether those complaints had merit. Amy left with the conviction that this center was resting on its past laurels and had, without recognizing it, slid into the danger zone of poor performance.

The last center Amy visited, led by a director who had been brought in from another agency about three years earlier, was a disaster. Complaints about its poor service were piling up not only at the center but at headquarters as well. Furthermore, the increasing stridency of the complaints was ringing alarm bells up and down the chain of command, even generating inquiries from congressional appropriators during budget hearings about the matter. In her interviews with center supervisors and employees, Amy discovered a seriously demoralized workforce led by a director who believed his job was to reduce operating costs before all else, resulting in cuts in everything from training to technology acquisition to customer outreach. Amy left convinced that this center required major reform.

Back at headquarters, Amy contemplated her strategy for improving and creating consistent performance at the three centers. She comprehended that in doing so she must use an approach that would preserve what was working while eliminating the causes for problematic performance. After all, the centers had to keep providing the support that the field offices required during this transition; she could not tolerate a severe drop in service levels. So Amy's challenge was a daunting one.

Confronting the Situation-Diagnosis Challenge

Different situations demand different strategies. But far too many new leaders do a poor job of diagnosing their situations and tailoring their strategies accordingly. They fall into the trap of assuming that one size will fit all and fail to recognize that different parts of their organizations may need to be approached in very different ways. When new leaders misread the situation of their new organizations, or just assume that an approach they had success with in the past will work again in their new assignment, they risk heading off in the wrong direction with a strategy that will likely backfire, not only causing a setback in realizing their mandates but also damaging their credibility. Fortunately, Amy avoided that pitfall.

At the same time, it is easy for new leaders to get overwhelmed by the complexity of a new organization and end up responding ad hoc to the host of different situations and problems they find. In response to the myriad challenges Amy faced, she could easily have adopted a very tactical approach, for example, and fought the many fires that so obviously were burning. But the result would have been a diffuse and incoherent approach that would not have yielded much in the way of traction.

To avoid these twin traps, new leaders like Amy need to find and tread the productive middle ground between "one size fits all" and "it depends on everything." This means having a framework for diagnosing the situation, identifying key types of situations, and drawing on an established repertoire of strategies for dealing with them. It also means figuring out which aspects of the work culture promote superior performance and which are dysfunctional and need to be changed.

Analyzing Your Situation

Whether you are assuming a senior executive position that substantially expands your area of leadership or are becoming a first-line supervisor over a function that may be undergoing change due to past performance problems or a new mission, it is essential to take steps to thoroughly understand the nature of the situation you are entering before making and implementing decisions. Doing your homework will enable you to achieve some credibility and so increase the likelihood of your longer-term success.

Like many management assignments in government, Amy Donovan's overall situation turned out to include aspects of three of the ST$_A$RS transition situations discussed in chapter 1.

- **Turnaround.** At least two of the centers fell into the turnaround category because they had troubling performance deficiencies that had to be corrected.

- **Realignment.** Because the existing structures and resource allocations did not promote efficiency or consistency in the delivery of important support services to departmental field offices, the situation presented elements of a realignment.

- **Sustaining success.** The situation featured sustaining-success characteristics because, irrespective of the centers' individual problems, they had strengths that had to be preserved and promulgated throughout the improvement process.

How does one decide which of the ST$_A$RS definitions best apply to the situation being faced? The process begins, as most roads to understanding do, with history. As illustrated in figure 2-1, organizations

FIGURE 2-1

The ST$_A$RS model

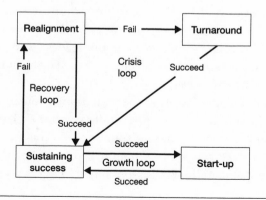

tend to move in predictable ways from one type of situation to another. For example, new organizations can grow and eventually become sustaining-success situations, which in turn create opportunities to launch new programs and initiatives in the *growth loop*.

But attaining such status does not guarantee continued success. Because of internal complacency or external challenges, or both, successful organizations tend to drift into trouble. Preventing this drift is especially difficult in governmental organizations, where authorizing statutes and imposed resource constraints often prevent implementing the kind of adaptive strategies that would keep organizational performance at the highest levels. Even if the organization is not yet in crisis, acute observers can see gathering storm clouds that signal the need for realignment.

Realigning an organization usually means redirecting its resources in a way that would return it to its previous sustaining-success state, designated in figure 2-1 as the *recovery loop*. Organizations are realigned by eliminating duplicate functions, employing new technologies, and reengineering work processes. Realignment often also means changing in fundamental ways the organization's strategy, structure, systems, skills, and even its culture. One of the main hurdles in developing a realignment strategy is that many organizations are in denial about their situations. They continue to believe they are sustaining success even though they are headed for trouble and resist efforts to change. But if efforts to realign fail, an organization will find itself facing a turnaround situation, which requires more dramatic action on a faster track with less regard for protecting the careers and status of the leaders who refused to acknowledge performance problems earlier. This is illustrated in figure 2-1 as the *crisis loop*.

Understanding the history of the organization you are now leading will help you grasp the opportunities and the challenges of your situation and better design your strategy. You cannot figure out where to take a new organization if you do not understand where it has been and how it got to where it is.

Identifying Challenges and Opportunities

As illustrated in table 2-1, each of the ST_ARS situations presents a distinct set of transition challenges and opportunities, and these have implications for the strategies new leaders should adopt.

TABLE 2-1

ST_ARS challenges and opportunities

Transition type	Challenges	Opportunities
Start-up	• Building structures and systems from scratch without a clear framework or boundaries. • Welding together a cohesive high-performing team. • Making do with limited resources.	• You can do things right from the beginning. • People are energized by the possibilities. • There is no preexisting rigidity in people's thinking.
Turnaround	• Reenergizing demoralized staff and other stakeholders. • Handling time pressure and having a quick and decisive impact. • Going deep enough with painful cuts.	• Everyone recognizes that change is necessary. • Affected constituencies may offer significant external support. • A little success goes a long way.
Realignment	• Dealing with deeply ingrained cultural norms that no longer contribute to high performance. • Convincing staff that change is necessary. • Restructuring the top team and refocusing the organization.	• The organization has significant pockets of strength. • People want to continue to see themselves as successful.
Sustaining success	• Avoiding decisions that cause problems. • Living in the shadow of a successful predecessor and dealing with the team he or she created. • Finding ways to take the organization to the next level.	• A strong team may already be in place. • People are motivated to succeed. • Foundations for continued success are in place.

In all of the four ST$_A$RS situations, the eventual goal is the same: a successful, high-performing organization. But each type of situation presents a distinct set of transition challenges. If you are in a start-up situation, you will be principally responsible for creating a new organization. In a turnaround situation you will need to decide on and implement radical change quickly. If you are entering a realignment situation, you will have to build awareness of the need for change among often recalcitrant subordinates. If you are in a sustaining-success situation, you may be inheriting an organization whose previous leader led it to become a high performer; the challenge will be to take charge in your own way while preserving what works well in the organization. Because the organization will most likely be older and more established, there also may be significant institutional constraints on what you can or cannot do.

Each situation also presents characteristic opportunities that you can leverage to build momentum. In start-ups you get to put the right foundation in place from the beginning; you don't have to deal with the legacy of others' choices, especially concerning personnel. In turnarounds everyone realizes that changes need to be made quickly, and that realization can help you move quickly. In both realignment and sustaining-success situations, the organizations involved often have significant strengths already, and you typically have more time before you must show results. That additional time is good news because in more-established organizations, you will have much to learn about the organizational culture and politics, and much to do to build supportive alliances.

The challenge of transforming the organization's psyche also varies in predictable ways, depending on which of the ST$_A$RS situations it is experiencing. As summarized in table 2-2, the prevailing mood in a start-up often is one of excited confusion. Your job is to channel that energy by putting in place the right vision, strategy, structures, and systems. In turnarounds you may be dealing with a group of people who are close to despair. Participants in a turnaround often know what the problems are but not what to do about them. It is your job to offer a light at the end of the tunnel. In realignments you will likely have to pierce through the veil of

TABLE 2-2

The psychological challenge

Transition type	Prevailing mood	Your challenge
Start-up	Confusion	Channeling their energy
Turnaround	Despair	Helping them overcome despair
Realignment	Denial	Piercing through their denial
Sustaining success	Complacency	Maintaining motivation

denial that is preventing people from confronting the need to re-invent their operation. Finally, in sustaining-success situations, you have to invent the challenge by finding ways to keep people motivated, to combat complacency, and to find new direction for growth—organizational and personal.

Clarifying Your Strategy Choices

Achieving clarity about the kind of situation you are entering enables you to decide what you need to do during the earliest part of your transition to your new leadership role. In particular, clarity helps you make four fundamental choices early on:

1. How much emphasis should you place on learning as opposed to doing?

2. How much emphasis should you place on offense versus defense?

3. What should you do to secure early wins?

4. Will you adopt a revolutionary or evolutionary approach to change?

Learning Versus Doing

How much time should you devote to deepening your understanding of the organization as opposed to making decisions, initiating

changes, reassigning people, and so on? The correct balance of learning and doing differs strikingly among the four ST_ARS situations. In
start-ups and turnarounds the premium is on doing; you have to make
some important early calls with imperfect information, and if you
spend too much time learning, you risk being overtaken by events.
Most assuredly, this is not to suggest that learning is unimportant in
these two situations. Rather, it is to suggest that the type of learning required in start-ups and turnarounds is fundamentally technical in
nature. It is about mastering quickly such technical aspects of the organization as its services or products, its constituencies, its proximity
to politically sensitive issues, its technologies, and so forth. Fortunately, this is the easiest and fastest type of learning.

In realignments or sustaining-success situations, a different emphasis on learning is warranted early on. Because you are dealing
with a group that believes it is already successful, it may not be
open to the need for change or for new direction from you. Early
changes—especially if they are perceived as threatening the organization's traditional strengths—will cost you dearly. That's the bad
news. The good news is that there is no need for early dramatic action in realignment or sustaining-success situations. In these cases
you have the time to delve deeply into the organizational culture
and politics before devising your agenda for improvement. Give
yourself permission to do so, and don't fall prey to the action imperative—thinking you have to act right away.

Offense Versus Defense

Early on, how much time should you invest in offensive planning (e.g., identifying new initiatives, developing new structures,
acquiring new technologies) and how much in playing good defense (e.g., protecting your organization's domain, strengthening
existing functions)? Certainly, you must do both in all situations,
but the relative emphasis you should place on offense and defense
differs greatly depending on how you see your particular situation.
For example, a start-up is all about offense: you are there to get
something underway, and there usually is nothing to defend. In a

turnaround, by contrast, the early imperative is a good defense: you need to identify the organization's remaining strengths and return focus to the defendable core so as to help acquire the resources needed to support your improvement agenda.

Realignments and sustaining-success situations differ comparably. In a realignment, the agenda is to make midcourse corrections that will remedy the slipping performance levels. In a sustaining-success situation, the key is to play good defense early on to avoid putting the organization's most valuable strengths at risk; over time, you may shift your attention to a strategy for tackling performance problems.

Securing Early Wins

To build momentum in your new job, you have to get some early wins. But what constitutes a win differs dramatically among the four ST_ARS situations. In a start-up getting the right team in place, acquiring needed resources, and achieving strategic focus represent key wins. Critically, you must decide what you are *not* going to do, and then discipline your organization not to do it. In turnarounds getting the right team in place is also a key potential early win, as is identifying the defendable core of the program and making major progress in redirecting energies to it. In realignments gaining acceptance of the need for change and instilling a sense of inevitability about it are often big early wins. And in sustaining-success situations gaining and displaying understanding and appreciation of what has made the organization successful is a key early win because it helps you earn the right to make decisions about the organization's future.

Revolution Versus Evolution

Finally, you must decide whether the situation demands a revolutionary approach to change or an evolutionary one.[1] The differences between the two approaches are illustrated in table 2-3. Turnarounds demand revolutionary change; change in a realignment situation is

TABLE 2-3

Change models

	Turnaround	Realignment
Rationale for change	• Urgency exists: the problem teaches the people	• Urgency must be created: the leader must teach the people
Change strategy	• Radical/visionary • Strategy/structure driven	• Incremental/planned • Process/skills driven
Leadership skills	• Directive/authority • Action orientation • Creating simplicity	• Consensus building/alliances • Learning orientation • Mastering complexity

necessarily and appropriately more about evolution than revolution. To put it another way, in turnarounds the problems teach people about the need for major changes. In realignments, by contrast, you must teach people about the problems.

Your approach to change has major implications for both strategy and leadership skills. Revolutionary change is best accomplished by defining a vision and a corresponding strategy and structure for implementing that strategy. It also demands a more directive leadership style and requires you to make tough calls with less than full knowledge and then adjust as you learn more. That directive leadership style and action orientation characteristic of entrepreneurial leaders are assets in this situation.

In evolutionary situations the urgency is less extreme; you have to teach people about the problem. More importantly, you have to take the time to understand the organization, its culture, and its politics so you can get the strategy right and build support for your plan. Too much emphasis on action early on is dangerous. An overly directive leadership style also is likely to create resistance. The patient consensus-building skills of a developmental leader are more likely to yield the desired results.

Because of leaders' differing imperatives, it is easy for those who prefer the revolutionary approach to stumble badly in realignment and sustaining-success situations and those who prefer the evolutionary approach to stumble in start-ups and turnarounds. The experienced turnaround person facing a realignment is at risk of arriving with "the answer" and moving too fast, needlessly causing resistance. The experienced realignment person in a turnaround situation is at risk of moving too slowly, expending energy on cultivating consensus when it is unnecessary to do so, thus squandering precious time.

This is not to say that people cannot be good at managing both revolutionary and evolutionary change. Good managers can succeed in doing either, though it is unusual for anyone to be equally good at both of them. It is essential to think hardheadedly about which of your skills and inclinations will serve you well in your particular situation and which are likely to get you into trouble.

At the same time, it is important to recognize that the challenges of public-sector leadership are disproportionately about managing evolutionary change. Based on our research, we estimate that the typical distribution of assignments in public-sector organizations is heavily skewed toward realignment and sustaining-success situations. Start-ups are the least common, and while turnaround can be found throughout government, they are still less frequently encountered than realignments or sustaining-success situations. The implication is that the vast majority of managers in the public sector have to be effective at managing evolution rather than fomenting revolution.

Leading Evolutionary Change

Leading change in realignment and sustaining-success situations turns out to be very hard, arguably harder than the more clear-cut, action-oriented challenges of starting up operations or turning them around. Key tools that developmental leaders use to pierce through denial and raise awareness of the need for change in their organizations are summarized below.

- **Listen actively.** Listening is a powerful tool for raising awareness of the need to change, especially if it is judiciously coupled with making observations and asking challenging questions.

- **Get others to educate your organization.** It is dangerous to be "the single point of pain" in making the case for change and easy to stimulate an immune-system reaction in your new organization where your ideas for change are rejected much as the human body mobilizes antibodies to defeat viral or bacterial invaders. To educate your organization more effectively and safely, involve others, such as your boss, customers, and key stakeholders in the process.

- **Change the metrics.** If the organization's metrics don't signal any problems, it is very difficult to make the case for change. If the problems really are there, then the metrics are likely to be the wrong ones. By changing the metrics, you can focus people on the emerging problems and help break down denial.

- **Engage in shared diagnosis.** Even if you are certain you understand "the problem," it rarely makes sense to share your diagnosis, lest you generate unnecessary resistance. Rather than trying to get people to embrace "the answer," it often is more effective to move them incrementally, starting with shared diagnosis. This approach is especially effective if the shared diagnosis involves getting people in the organization into dialogue with customers and key stakeholders.

- **Secure early wins and celebrate success.** To build momentum in promising directions, you should seek some early wins and then celebrate these successes. Focus on problems that are significant but tractable, and figure out how to make some early progress. Involve others whom you believe are aware of the need for change in these efforts, and celebrate triumphs when they happen.

- **Analyze and shape incentives.** Do a careful analysis of the incentives of influential people in the organization. What are they encouraged to do and not to do? Then focus on how you can alter these incentives by elevating and rewarding people who exemplify the right behaviors and by sanctioning, in reasonable ways, those who don't.

Although the situation Amy Donovan faced presented elements of three ST_ARS categories, by recognizing that it was primarily a realignment she was able to fashion a strategy to pierce through the denial that permeated each center. Both Amy and her bosses recognized that all three centers, even the worst-performing one, had certain strengths that had to be preserved; accordingly, performance improvements had to be designed and implemented in ways that did not interrupt the delivery of important support services.

Just into her second month as national director, Amy sought and quickly received from her bosses the authorization to institute an evolutionary strategy for improving the centers' performance. An important element of her strategy was the reassignment of the center directors to headquarters to act as her assistants in creating more cohesive standards of performance, and the appointment of three acting directors who predictably saw it in their best interest to support the performance-improvement effort.

Two of the three directors assigned to headquarters to assist Amy did not remain in their new positions for very long. The longest-serving of the directors retired rather than relocate, and the one who had been recruited from outside the agency a few years earlier requested reassignment after a highly dissatisfying year at headquarters. The third former center director, however, remained and became a valuable resource of institutional knowledge for Amy as she set out to realign resources among the centers, to redesign each center's performance standards to reflect new customer service and cost-control goals, and to develop new organizational structures that would allow cross-training among staff specialists. Ultimately, he was promoted and became Amy's deputy.

As a first step toward implementing her plan, Amy enlisted the three acting center directors to commission customer surveys, with the results going to each acting director and to Amy. The surveys highlighted responsiveness and quality issues as well as low levels of confidence that field offices had in their respective centers. From her early learning, Amy had a good sense of how the surveys would turn out and planned to present them in meetings at each center and to use them in the next step in the performance-improvement process: getting each center's staff to abandon their complacency and demoralization and confront the reality of their performance and what needed to be done about it to improve work processes. Amy's plan was to parlay these discussions into the next phase—namely, how to retain and share those practices that were working and discard those that were not. From there, after establishing a relatively clear sense of the problem, the difficult issues of how to implement the performance-improvement plan without degrading service levels could be addressed.

Diagnosing Your ST$_A$RS Portfolio

Having used the ST$_A$RS model to diagnose your overall situation, the next step is to drill deeper and assess the state of your overall responsibilities. This means taking time to analyze your responsibilities in terms of a portfolio using the ST$_A$RS framework: What part of your job responsibilities involves starting up something new? Turning around something in trouble? Realigning something before a crisis occurs? Sustaining the success of something that is and continues to be strong?

The following exercise will help you think systematically about challenges and opportunities in each component of your organization. It will also provide you with a common language with which to talk to your new team about why and how you are going to manage various components differently.

The starting point for doing this portfolio analysis is to decide how you will break down your job responsibilities. Divide your job responsibilities up into distinct categories:

- Services provided

- Projects

- Processes

- Facilities and locations

- People and groups

The next step is to divide your responsibilities up in terms of the ST$_A$RS categories using the grid shown in figure 2-2. What parts belong in the start-up cell? The turnaround cell? The realignment cell? The sustaining-success cell?

Now step back and look at the mix. What are the implications for what you need to do in the various parts of your portfolio? What are the implications for the mix of entrepreneurial and developmental skills you need to employ and where you need to employ them?

Note also that the ST$_A$RS portfolio tool can be a powerful aid in gaining consensus with bosses and direct reports about the situation and the implications for priorities and strategy. In Amy Donovan's case, as soon as she made her diagnosis of the situation she faced in

FIGURE 2-2

Analyzing ST$_A$RS portfolios

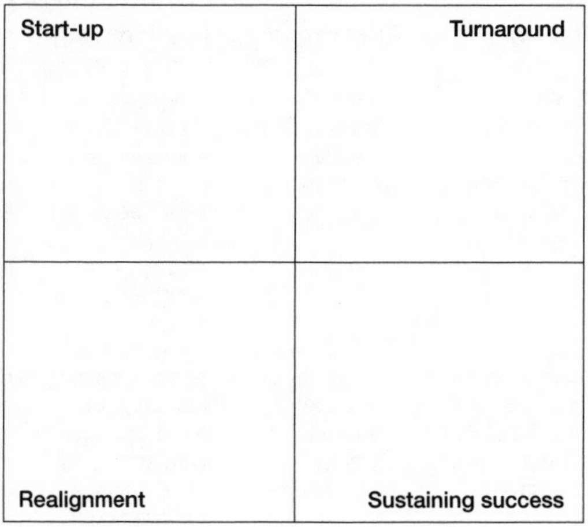

Start-up	Turnaround
Realignment	Sustaining success

improving performance at the three centers, she shared it with the boss and gained his concurrence. This enabled her to proceed with confidence in implementing the performance-improvement strategy she developed. The lesson is clear: you want to avoid playing the lone hero, especially when facing a challenge as difficult as the one Amy faced. The earlier you can share your assessment of the situation with your bosses and get their concurrence on it as well as on your ensuing strategy for carrying out your mandate, and the earlier you can enlist the participation of key staff, the better off you will be.

To do all this, it's crucial to adjust for your level. In government the specific management tasks necessary for success vary among the four ST$_A$RS situations as well as between the middle and senior levels of management, as summarized in table 2-4. Bureaucracies of all kinds, especially those in the public sector that are constructed from somewhat rigid statutes and regulations, feature fairly clearly drawn lines of authority and spheres of responsibility. The

TABLE 2-4

Managerial responsibilities

	Start-up	Turnaround	Realignment	Sustaining success
Middle management	Rapidly calculate resource requirements and mobilize workforce.	Rapidly institute prescribed corrective measures.	Diagnose barriers to improvement, institute changes within function, and provide feedback.	Assess operation, seek new challenges to better performance, and lead improvement process.
Senior management	Rapidly set goals, acquire authorities and resources, and make decisions on strategy.	Quickly decide cause of prior performance failure and corrective action needed.	Grasp culture/politics, formulate improvement strategy with staff, and build supporting alliances.	Grasp culture/politics, create new challenges, and build alliances of supporters.

result is a mixture of management tasks that, while neatly laid out on paper, may overlap in practice, causing confusion and conflict. To avoid potential problems, leaders must clearly communicate the definition of the situation faced throughout management.

Because of the differing tasks and corresponding skill sets needed to carry them out, middle- and senior-level managers who do not understand the nature of the situation they face may easily choose a wrongly constructed approach, creating conflict and impeding performance. For example, the leader who misreads a realignment for a turnaround is at risk of arriving with "the answer" and moving too fast, needlessly causing resistance. The corollary is the leader who misdiagnoses a turnaround as a realignment and moves too slowly, expending energy on cultivating consensus when quicker action is needed. Of course, this is not to say that a leader with start-up or turnaround experience cannot also succeed in realignments or sustaining-success situations, or vice versa; it simply is necessary to think carefully about which of your skills and predilections will serve best in your new situation, and which might lead you down the wrong path right at the start.

Conclusion

Adeptly matching strategy to situation is critical to getting off to the right start in transitioning to a new leadership role. Which of the four ST_ARS situations are you facing? What are the implications of identifying a predominant situation for the challenges and opportunities you are likely to confront and for how you should approach your transition? What are the implications for your learning agenda? Which of your skills and strengths are likely to be most valuable in your new situation, and which might get you into difficulty? What is the organization's prevailing frame of mind? Should your early focus be on offense or defense? And finally, what is the mixture of ST_ARS situations in your portfolio of organizational components?

Amy Donovan did an excellent job of understanding and answering each of these key questions and reaffirming her mandate with her boss before taking off with a strategy to improve the performance of the three support centers. That was the key to her success.

ACCELERATION CHECKLIST

1. What mix of the four ST_ARS situations are you facing—start-up, turnaround, realignment, or sustaining success? Use the ST_ARS portfolio tool to define and prioritize your responsibilities.

2. What are the implications for the challenges and opportunities you are likely to confront and for how you should approach accelerating your transition?

3. What are the implications for your learning agenda? Do you only need to understand the technical side of the organization, or is it critical that you understand culture and politics as well?

4. Which of your skills and strengths are likely to be most valuable in your new situation, and which have the potential to get you into trouble?

5. What is the prevailing frame of mind? What psychological transformations do you need to make, and how will you bring them about?

6. Should your early focus be on offense or defense?

Accelerate Your Learning

W HEN SANDRA MARTIN, an engineer with fifteen
years' experience in a major federal research
agency, received a call from the agency director
asking her to come back to headquarters to help straighten out
some problems that had arisen with a major engineering effort,
she was more than ready to make the move. She was at the end of a
two-year special assignment at an agency field office where she had
put together a cooperative research program with several regional
universities. While she had met her mandate of successfully negotiating with participating universities and opening up the closed culture of the agency research staff, she was ready to get back into
engineering. Just one week after receiving the call, Sandra reported
to headquarters to assume the role of interim program manager of
a highly classified and politically sensitive R&D effort. Sandra expected to be in her post temporarily until a new manager—one
with direct experience with the program—was named, and she was
quite surprised when she was offered the position permanently
after just two months.

Sandra was selected because of the excellent management cre-
dentials had she established in her previous assignment, which, as
an engineer working with scientists, she likened to herding cats.

The program Sandra inherited had just experienced a major crisis. Three months earlier a major milestone had been missed due to serious flaws in the design and quality-control processes instituted by Sandra's predecessor (who was removed as a result), precipitating a major budget crisis, bringing embarrassment to the agency director and his supporters, and generating impatient scrutiny from several congressional committees.

Sandra's mandate, as explained to her by the agency director, was to correct the problems with the design and quality-control processes that had led to the blown milestone and get the program back on track by the next milestone date, less than one year away. This directive thrust Sandra into perhaps the most visible and critical position in her agency at the time. But aside from the intense public scrutiny and substantial technical issues involved, Sandra faced several major challenges in navigating a political and cultural minefield within the agency itself.

Sandra was promoted over the project's chief engineer, Bill Thompson, who had expected to be selected as the new manager. She, in fact, had advocated for Bill's promotion to project manager but now, to her surprise, found herself as his boss and needed to figure out how to gain his support. Complicating matters further, the 150-member team Sandra inherited was in a serious state of disarray. Her predecessor was a tyrant who used intimidation to get results and effectively disenfranchised the staff by making important technical decisions without their input. Because of this, Sandra needed to quickly learn the capabilities, commitment level, and motivation of each key staff member.

Finally, the project as a whole lacked the kind of structure and accountability that was needed to carry out the mandate assigned by the agency director. Sandra's top priority, therefore, was to reshape the staff from a loosely organized group of specialists to a focused, coordinated team with a common sense of purpose and a stake in the outcome. Creating such structure would mean removing some staff members from the project, a delicate task that had to be done in a way that would boost, not damage, the already-fragile morale of her new team.

Approaching the Learning Challenge

Like Sandra, you may be assuming leadership of a major program. Or you may be taking over a staff function or even leading a complete agency. Regardless, you should strive during your first few weeks to learn as much as you can about challenges, resources, and barriers. This is easy to say, but to get up the learning curve fast, you have to be both pragmatic about what you need to learn and focused in how you go about learning it so as to avoid early missteps that could sap your energy and undermine your credibility.

Sandra, for example, had to plow through mountains of technical material, come to know and assess a demoralized and disgruntled staff, establish constructive working relationships with a vast number of contractors, gain an understanding of the mechanics of political intrigue within and surrounding the agency, and, on top of all that, adapt to an extremely high-public-profile agency with accompanying media interest. If she did not quickly organize her learning process, she knew she would soon become buried and immobilized by an avalanche of information.

Learning about a new position can feel like drinking from a fire hose. There often is simply far too much information to absorb about the programs that now are under your control, the rules and regulations that apply to them, the strategies and policies of political appointees or senior executives to whom you report, and—critically—the people whom you will supervise or with whom you must form working relationships. Amid the mountain of information facing you, it is easy to miss important signals. Far more than any other phase of your new position, the transition period demands efficiency and effectiveness in learning. As illustrated in figure 3-1, achieving success will help create a *virtuous cycle:* effective learning will lead to good early decisions, which will help build credibility. If you fail, you could set up a vicious cycle that will make it increasingly difficult to get things done.[1]

During Sandra's first few months on the job, her primary leadership task was to diagnose her situation. She divided her time between tackling technical learning and assessing and assembling

FIGURE 3-1

Virtuous cycles

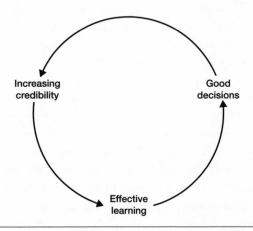

her team. One of her very first acts of team building was to convene an all-hands meeting and publicly state that she had advocated the promotion of Bill Thompson to the position she now held and was herself surprised to have been appointed to it. She praised his past contributions and stressed his importance to achieving their new mandate. However, as she made clear, "We are here now, and we must make this work." This meeting, and Bill's reciprocal show of support, was an important and big step toward establishing her credibility with team members. (Sandra later nominated Bill for one of the agency's highest awards.)

Despite a heavy travel schedule to contractor and agency sites and a mountain of technical reports to digest, Sandra met with each key team member over the next few weeks to learn about their responsibilities and how they had been carrying those responsibilities out under her predecessor. She instituted regular staff meetings and technical issue meetings, insisting that they be held even if team members thought they were not needed at a particular time, and established an accountability policy requiring that all parties sign off on technical decisions made at those meetings. She demonstrated the value of such structured meetings when one issue, thought to be minor, turned out to be more involved than originally thought. It was the absence of this kind of participative structure that may have led to the technical failures responsible for the missed milestone.

In her second month, with the direct and influential involvement of the staff, Sandra devised a reorganization and resource plan that would substantially increase the team's staffing level as well as better focus its efforts. When the plan was quickly approved by the agency director, Sandra not only won the respect of her new team but, because of the participative way she prepared the plan, she gained their commitment. The project staff, once a maligned and seriously despondent group following the missed milestone, was turned around by outstanding leadership in a time of crisis and successfully met the next milestone on time and under budget.

Avoiding Learning Missteps

Sandra was effective in connecting with her organization early on largely because she avoided some classic learning traps into which new leaders often fall. For example, too many new leaders either arrive in their new positions with "the answer"—a preordained fix for the organization's problems—or reach conclusions too early in their tenures. New leaders fall into this trap through arrogance or insecurity, or because they believe they must appear decisive and establish a directive tone.[2] But staff members become cynical when they perceive that leaders are dealing superficially with what they see as deep problems. When people believe their leaders' minds are made up, they are understandably reticent to share information.

Other new leaders take the time to learn but focus on the wrong things by drifting onto a risky course of self-fulfilling learning. Self-fulfilling learning means avoiding venturing into new areas and instead restricting your acquisition of information to the boundaries of your previous experience and training. This is natural—but also very dangerous, because to focus on learning about the aspects of the organization that you feel equipped to understand and to avoid those that you don't is likely to leave you with a serious knowledge deficit. If you have a strong technical orientation, for example, you will be well equipped to learn about technical challenges in the new job, which is fine if those are the most important issues. But, as Sandra Martin realized, if the real challenges also lie in culture and politics, you could find yourself strolling through a minefield blindfolded.

Planning to Learn

In an ideal world, a newly appointed manager like Sandra would have several weeks before entering the position to become familiar with the new organization, to engage in discussions with the new boss, and to gain a sense of what accomplishments might be expected and what resources might be obtainable to help achieve them. Regrettably, new leaders seldom have the luxury of such an orientation period. Our research has shown that the time between selection and placement in government is as short as one or two days, and rarely longer than one or two weeks. Moreover, when a new manager comes from another agency or, more commonly, moves from a specialty into a more general management position, there usually is little available in the way of advanced warning or instruction. Accordingly, new managers often find themselves pretty much left to their own devices to acquire the knowledge necessary to get a good understanding of what they will be facing in their new jobs.

To succeed in doing this, you have to plan to learn. You may be tempted to simply dive in and try to absorb the information available to you. You should resist that temptation. Take the time to sketch out your learning agenda. What are the most important questions you need to get answered? What are the most important hypotheses you need to test? Only by identifying *what* you need to learn (your learning agenda) can you figure out *how* you will most efficiently and effectively go about learning it (your learning plan).

Establishing Your Learning Agenda

When Sandra Martin assumed leadership of the program, she understood that she faced a tremendous learning task. Although the learning challenge you may face in your new leadership role may not be as complex or as high profile as Sandra's, approaching it in a disciplined fashion is every bit as important to your success as it was to hers. You cannot learn everything all at once, if ever, so you need to structure your learning according to what is most critical. Also, it is important to accept that you may not "get" everything the first time around; don't resist reaching out for help—it will not make you seem unprepared or unqualified.

Learning as an Investment Process

You should approach your efforts to get up to speed as an investment process, and your time and energy as assets to be carefully managed. You are not learning for its own sake; rather, you are seeking *actionable insights,* or knowledge that will enable you to figure out what you need to do. Sandra Martin took the time to realistically assess the learning challenge before her and approached them in an orderly way that yielded very positive early results for her, her team, and her agency. To maximize your return on investment in learning, you too have to effectively and efficiently extract actionable insights from the mass of information—and the corollary situation of no information—that often awaits new leaders. You can do this by asking questions—about the past, the present, and the future. Why are things done the way they are? Are those reasons still valid today? Are conditions changing such that something different should be done in the future?

Learning with a Point of View

While there is virtue in keeping an open mind, a new leader should not disregard his or her experience when approaching a new learning challenge. Many people in government who have been selected for a leadership position have advanced in specialized careers before being put in charge and, accordingly, have had the opportunity to make mental notes along the way about what they would do if they were the boss. So now you are, and here is your chance to try out some of your ideas for effective leadership. A learning agenda that is shaped by a point of view developed before entry is far preferable to following a learning script suggested by others or, at worst, to random information gathering. This is most definitely not to say that you should have your mind made up about what is important to know and what is not. But entering a new leadership position with some hypotheses rooted in your experience about the best way to handle your new assignment enables you to focus your questions and better utilize the answers to test your ideas about what should come first.

There are risks, of course, to approaching learning with a point of view. The danger is that you will be guided by assumptions, which tend to go untested, instead of hypotheses, which demand testing. As one leader we interviewed put it, "I think of a hypothesis as a work in progress, as opposed to an assumption, which is a more fixed position that you are trying to validate." Communicating to staff members when discussing your plans that you are merely testing ideas and stimulating discussion rather than formulating concrete plans or making personnel decisions will help ease their natural apprehension and confusion about your intent.

Technical, Political, and Cultural Learning

In putting together your learning agenda, it helps to have a framework for identifying high-leverage questions and hypotheses. Many new leaders have found it helpful to use three lenses to diagnose their organizations—technical, political, and cultural.[3]

Technical Learning. Mastering the nature and key features of the organization's products, services, and customers composes technical learning. This terminology, once most relevant to business organizations, has come into common usage in governments at all levels over the past decade or so. Viewing end users of your agency's products or services as customers and legitimate stakeholders in the quality with which these products or services are delivered has had a transforming effect on how government managers design their organizations and evaluate their effectiveness. This is as true inside an organization as it is in direct dealings with taxpayers, legislators, and political leaders. Understanding the connection between what your organization does every day and what its constituency expects or requires must be a primary item on your learning agenda.

Political Learning. Every organization is political—factions, power struggles, negotiations, and coalition-building efforts can be found in any large human enterprise. In government, however, the political environment is complicated by overt partisan competition, election results that can dramatically affect the authorities and policies under which government agencies operate, high transparency, and a large and frequently contentious set of stakeholders. Though these factors play most upon the senior levels of an agency or on those agency functions that deal most directly with public constituencies, the political universe within which government agencies operate also affects the way internal functions perform. For the new manager, learning how decisions are made, identifying whom to consult, recognizing influential coalitions (especially those whose support you will require), and developing a keen sense of policy imperatives are keys to achieving good political positioning when it comes to competition for staff, money, and other critical resources.

Cultural Learning. Culture is at the core of the organization and influences the other four dimensions of organizational architecture—strategy, structure, systems, and skills—and shapes the thinking behind each. Indeed, the most important leadership problems you are likely to face in your new situation will have a significant cultural dimension.

Culture has been defined as a set of shared expectations.[4] Your organization's culture consists of the norms and values that shape team members' behavior, attitudes, and expectations and cues them about what to do and not do. Often, as discussed earlier, there are fundamental assumptions about how things work that are so embedded and long standing in an organization that people are not even aware of their existence. So it is critical that you diagnose problems in your group's existing culture and address them early. Only then can the culture fully support the group strategy and align smoothly with the other pieces of the group architecture—structure, systems, and skills.

Cultures within organizations or groups develop over time and, because they are deeply rooted, can form a strong protective barrier around the status quo. (See "The Origins of Bureaucratic Culture.") In some cases you may learn that certain aspects of the culture are highly functional and worthy of preservation; in others you may discover they are impediments to high performance and must be

---

The Origins of Bureaucratic Culture

The fundamental conception of a bureaucratic institution, as developed in the later nineteenth century and still largely maintained, is that an organization is governed by rules rather than cultural norms. But what this purist model fails to take into consideration is the autonomy of the individuals who compose the organization, particularly that their actions are influenced by many factors, only one of which is bureaucratic rules. Perhaps the most critical role played by any leader, especially those at an organization's highest levels, is one of interpretation; the rules may provide a framework within which to act, but they do not by themselves dictate decisions. Leaders, as well as all those others on their influence maps, are social beings and act beyond the specifications of rule sets. They have prejudices, interests, and fears in the same way that any individual has, and these factors, together with the prevailing cultural norms of the wider society, will influence how people work within the rule-governed framework.

Therefore, it is important to realize that an organization's culture more than its rules will serve to shape how it approaches *new* problems, problems not dealt with within the extant structure. Organization charts and rule books are static and serve mainly to shape the present; they have little to say about how a bureaucracy should face new challenges and problems. So the people who must face those kinds of problems—the organization's leaders—will inevitably be most guided by cultural norms in devising their strategies. In this sense, culture starts where rules leave off.

---

changed. In either case, it is vital to diagnose the existing culture and learn how to capitalize on its strengths and address its problems.

To understand your group's culture, you must peer beneath the surface-level signals, such as styles of dress and ways of communicating and interacting, as well as the social norms, or shared rules that guide behavior, and explore the various work-specific mindsets that exist within the organization. For example, do people seem more interested in individual accomplishment and reward, or are they more focused on group performance? Do they show up to meetings on time? Do they seem engaged? Do they have a clear commitment to achieving results? The answers to such questions can provide important actionable insights to help you invest your learning time and energy with the best potential return in terms of developing an organizational culture that is supportive rather than indifferent or resistant to your goals.

A new leader should search beyond surface-level signals for the deepest assumptions group members take for granted. For a new leader who is trying to align the various dimensions of his or her group behind a new strategy, the most relevant assumptions involve the following:

- **Power.** Who do employees believe can legitimately make decisions and exert influence?

- **Value.** What actions and outcomes do employees believe create value? Value can take such forms as efficiency and effectiveness in delivering the product or service, satisfying the users of the product or service, promoting innovation, creating a supportive working environment, and so forth.

How do you tease out fundamental assumptions? To understand assumptions about power, learn how decisions were made in the past and determine who deferred to whom. To understand assumptions about value, look at how people spend their time and what energizes them most. For example, do employees seem to focus most on forging positive working relationships with each other? Is efficiency valued? Are they mindful of how their products or services meet or fall short of users' expectations?

During your first months on the new job, you cannot hope to do more than diagnose the culture and begin working on changing its most troubling aspects. Following are five ways to begin the process of cultural change; whichever ones you decide to use, aim for changes that will align with your group's strategy, structure, systems, and skills.

1. **Change performance metrics and incentives.** In public-sector organizations, metrics and incentive systems usually take the form of rules imposed by statute, regulation, or broad policy directives and are not easily changed, so focus on linking the agency's performance-evaluation system and specific individual performance requirements to the group's strategy.

2. **Set up pilot projects.** Form multidisciplinary task forces to provide employees opportunities to experiment with new tools, technologies, and work processes to solve ongoing group performance problems.

3. **Bring in new people.** Again, this is not so easy in public-sector organizations governed by rigid personnel ceilings and other hiring or budgetary restrictions. But when it's possible, integrating a new specialist with unique expertise, for example, can wind up stimulating new thinking and elevating the performance level of the entire group.

4. **Promote collective learning.** Expose group members to new ways of operating through the use of benchmarking.[5]

5. **Engage in collective visioning.** Find creative ways to bring people together, such as off-site meetings to brainstorm ideas for a process improvement and envision new approaches to doing things.

For Sandra, assuming leadership of a troubled, high-profile program within her agency demanded rapid cultural learning to avoid costly missteps that could set the organization back even further. Her past experience within the agency was an asset in this regard, but there was much that she did not know about the intricate interpersonal relationships in her new group. This is where her systematic and inclusive approach to learning paid off, not only in the early acquisition of crucial knowledge but also in beginning the process of reorienting the staff toward a new way of operating.

Getting Started

How should you compile your early list of guiding questions? Start by generating your initial list of questions about the past, the present, and the future. The "Diagnostic Template" offers sample questions in these three categories. Use it to develop your own list of questions to focus your early learning.

Diagnostic Template

Questions About the Past

Performance

- How has this organization performed in the past? How do people in the organization think it has performed?

- How were goals set? Were they set too low or too high?

- Were internal or external benchmarks used?

- What measures were employed to assess performance? What behaviors did they encourage and discourage?

- What happened if goals were not met?

Root Causes

- If performance has been good, why has that been the case?

- What have been the relative contributions of the organization's strategy, structure, technical capabilities, culture, and politics?

- If performance has been poor, why has that been the case? Do the primary issues reside in the organization's strategy? structure? technical capabilities? culture? politics?

---

continued

History of Change

- What efforts have been made to change the organization? What happened?

- Who has been instrumental in shaping this organization? Who have been the heroes and the villains in this organization's narrative? What does that say about what is valued and not valued?

Questions About the Present

Mission, Vision, and Strategy

- What are the stated mission, vision, and strategy of the organization?

- Is it really pursuing the stated strategy? If not, why not? If so, is the strategy going to take the organization where it needs to go?

People

- Who is capable and who is not?

- Who can be trusted and who cannot? Who is open and who is secretive?

- Who has influence and why?

Stakeholders

- Who are the key external stakeholders? What do they expect the organization to do? What would they like it to do?

- What other individuals and groups could have influence on the way the organization functions?

Processes

- What are the key service delivery and support processes of the organization? Who are the "customers" and who are the "suppliers"?

- Are these performing acceptably in terms of quality, reliability, and timeliness? If not, why not?

Early Wins

- With which people or relationships can you achieve some early wins?

- In what processes can you earn early wins?

Questions About the Future

Challenges and Opportunities

- In what areas is the organization likely to face stiff challenges in the coming year? What can be done now to prepare for those challenges?

- What are the most promising unexploited opportunities? What would need to happen to realize their potential?

Barriers and Resources

- What are the most formidable barriers to making needed changes?

- Are there islands of excellence or other high-quality resources that you can leverage?

- What new capabilities need to be developed?

Predictable Surprises

- What lurking landmines could detonate and push you off track?

- Are there critical external relationships that must be repaired?

- What potentially damaging cultural or political missteps must you avoid making?

Culture

- Which elements of the culture should be preserved?

- Which elements need to change?

You should also spend some time writing your learning agenda down. Just as establishing a formal process of assessing individual performance is important to the effectiveness of an organization, so is it important to you as a new leader as a way to make your learning agenda a living, evolving plan for self-development. Recognize that as time passes new questions and hypotheses will be added as others are answered, and keep a record of your learning goals as a way of being accountable to yourself for the success of your transition. Make it a part of your weekly discipline to reassess those goals, test their relevance to the current situations you face, and, as necessary, reformulate them to bring them into better alignment with the challenges ahead.

Creating a Learning Plan

Your learning agenda defines *what* you need to learn; your learning plan specifies *how* you will do it by translating learning goals into specific sets of actions that should constitute the primary focus of your first few weeks in your new position. Translating the goals enumerated in your learning agenda into a plan of action can be accomplished in two basic steps: identifying the best sources of knowledge and learning systematically.

Identify the Best Sources of Knowledge

Identifying the most promising sources of information about your organization will make your learning more efficient and effective. Acquiring actionable insights requires both delving into documentary sources—such as budgets, operations manuals, regulation books, procedural and policy issuances, and mission and strategic statements—and engaging with human sources both within and beyond your immediate staff. But some documents and some people have more to teach you than others, so to avoid spending time fruitlessly and slowing the pace of your learning, examine your new organization from five distinct points of view:

- **From the outside in.** This calls for becoming acquainted with budget and recent key policy and procedural directives affecting the performance of your function, and consulting with the users of your services or products, your suppliers, and others who interact with your organization. If you are heading a unit within a larger organization, it will be appropriate to consult with internal customers and suppliers. How does each perceive your organization? What do they see as its strengths? Its weaknesses?

- **From the inside out.** This calls for becoming acquainted with key internal operating directives, as well as staff personnel files, and consulting with people in your organization who deal directly with the users of your services or products and other stakeholders. How do internal people and other stakeholders perceive the reputation of your organization among those with whom they interact? What do they see as its strengths? Its weaknesses? What problems do they mention that others in the organization do not? If their impressions do not match what your external sources told you, what do you think accounts for the discrepancy?

- **From the bottom up.** This calls for consulting with working-level specialists in key functions within your organization. How do they perceive the organization? What do they see as its strengths? Its weaknesses? What problems do they report that others don't? Are they clear on key policy and procedural issues and on important quality standards?

- **From the top down.** This calls for becoming acquainted with mission and strategic statements issued by top executives, and consulting with senior managers. How do these high-level players perceive your organization? What do they see as its strengths? Its weaknesses? What problems do they observe that others don't? Do their perceptions match those of people further down in the organization? If not, why not?

- **Sideways from the middle.** This calls for consulting with people in integrator roles within the larger organization, such as project and program leaders, heads of relevant task forces or working groups, and those who perform informal liaison tasks between functional units. How do these people perceive your organization? What do they see as its strengths? Its weaknesses? What problems do they discern that others do not?

Learn Systematically

When Sandra Martin was unexpectedly thrust into the hot seat of fixing one of the most critical problems facing her agency at the time, one of the first things she addressed was what she *did not* know. As an engineer, trained and experienced in rational problem solving, Sandra approached the technical, political, and cultural learning challenges she faced by reaching out in an open and systematic way that enabled her to accelerate progress on all fronts. But you do not have to be an engineer to formulate a plan for efficient learning. All it takes is a little focus.

Once you're armed with a learning agenda and an awareness of high-leverage sources of insight, the next step is to determine what approaches you should use to learn in the most efficient and effective way. This means focusing on extracting the maximum insight from one-on-one meetings with high-potential sources. The core of your plan is a cyclical learning process in which you collect, analyze, and distill information, and develop and test hypotheses, thus deepening your understanding of your new organization and accelerating the rate of your overall learning.

Listening Actively

Getting the most out of one-on-one meetings requires that you engage in the art of *active listening*.[6] Your objectives in doing this are both to learn and to be seen as genuinely seeking more insight. Listening, simply but intensely, is itself a powerful form of persuasion.

To engage in effective active listening, you should adopt the following guidelines:

- **Pose questions that stimulate reflective responses.** Avoid questions with yes/no answers and ones that provoke knee-jerk restatements of positions or defensive reactions. "Why are you so opposed to a system the organization needs so much?" is not a good question. "I understand that you are worried about our capacity to absorb a new system right now—can you tell me more about your concerns?" is much better. Always take the time to write out a few good questions before each meeting.

- **Triangulate on key issues.** Ask the same basic question in two or three different ways (not all at once, of course, but over the course of the meeting) to see how consistent the answers are. By doing this, you often can elicit additional, hidden concerns. Of course you need to be careful in doing this—you don't want to appear as if you don't believe what you are hearing or aren't listening!

- **Summarize and test comprehension.** Repeat back what you are hearing to both demonstrate that you have been listening and understand the other person's perspective and to test that you really have. Note that summarizing and testing comprehension rapidly bleeds over into active persuasion, so be careful you don't take it too far. No one likes having his or her statements twisted or caricatured.

- **Use what-ifs to probe the depth of opposition.** Statements of the form, "If x were to be true, would it allay your concerns?" can help you gain deeper insight into the nature and depth of restraining forces. Here, too, active listening opens a door to persuasion. If done well, listening can transform a positional exchange into a dialogue on what it would take to go down the road you desire.

- **Watch for hot-button reactions.** As you ask questions and repeat back what you have learned, look carefully for what generates strong emotional reactions because such reactions also can provide insight into restraining forces. Judiciously probe these reactions, perhaps by making leading statements such as, "You seem to feel strongly about that . . ." But, once again, be careful not to trigger defensive reactions unnecessarily.

As you engage in active listening and seek to gain actionable insights, you should take care not to fall into two common traps. The first, discussed previously, is to engage in self-fulfilling learning. The second trap, also already mentioned, is to inadvertently trigger defensive reactions, causing the other party to become even more committed to his or her position and unwilling to explore value-creating solutions. So watch out for defensive body language (e.g., the crossing of arms or legs, pushing back from the table or desk), and if you observe some, back off and give the person a chance to recover and reengage.

Employing Structured Methods

Active listening is the foundation of effective learning. It enables you to extract the maximum insight from each interaction. But you can further enhance your learning effectiveness by being systematic about the order in which you engage in one-on-one interactions. This means using horizontal slices, vertical slices, and interface triangulation to gain actionable insight.

Horizontal slices are a series of meetings with people at the same level of the organization. It's as if you took a knife and sliced through the structure at a specific level. Your goal in doing this is to probe how opinion and insight vary at that level.

To interview systematically, you should develop a common template of questions you will ask all the people you interview in the "slice." The reason to compile these questions is to provide structure for your subsequent analysis and reflection. That way, the responses you get are comparable. You can line them up side by side and analyze what is consistent and inconsistent about the responses. Otherwise, you risk being overly influenced by the first person you talk with (which researchers in the field of social influence call the "primacy effect") or the last person you talk with (the "recency effect"). Using one set of questions also helps you gain insight into which people are being more or less open.

To illustrate the idea of horizontal slices, imagine that you plan to meet with your direct reports to elicit their assessments of the organization. How might you go about doing this? Bringing them together right away might be a mistake because some will hesitate to reveal their views in a public forum. Instead, you could talk with them one-on-one, taking into consideration whether you should meet with your direct reports in a particular order.

A good template for conducting these meetings might consist of brief opening remarks about yourself and your approach, followed by questions about the other person (background, family, and interests) and then a standard set of questions about the organization, such as the ones outlined below:

- What are the biggest challenges the organization is facing (or will face in the near future)?

- Why is the organization facing (or going to face) these challenges?

- What are the most promising unexploited opportunities for improvement?

- What would need to happen for the organization to exploit the potential of these opportunities?

- If you were leading this organization, what would you focus attention on?

These five questions, coupled with careful listening and thoughtful follow-up, are certain to elicit many insights. By asking everyone the same set of questions, you can identify prevalent and divergent views and thus avoid being swayed by the first, most forceful, or most articulate person you talk to.

How people answer can also tell you a lot about your new team and its politics. Who answers directly, and who is evasive or prone to going on tangents? Who takes responsibility, and who points fingers? Who has a broad view of the organization, and who seems stuck in a silo?

Once you have distilled these early discussions into a set of observations, questions, and insights, convene your direct reports as a group, give your impressions and questions, and invite some discussion. You will learn more about both the key challenges the organization is facing and nature of team dynamics by doing so and will simultaneously demonstrate how quickly you have begun to identify key issues.

You need not follow this process rigidly. You could, for example, get an outside consultant to do some diagnosis of the organization and share the results with your group. Or you could invite an internal facilitator to run the process. The point is that even a modest amount of structure—a script and a sequence of interactions such as meeting with people individually, doing some analysis, and then meeting as a group—can dramatically accelerate your ability to extract actionable insights. Naturally, the questions you will ask will be tailored specifically for the groups you meet.

Vertical slices are a series of meetings with people at different levels of the organization. The basic process is similar to that used for horizontal slices. You identify a good sample of people at different levels and ask them similar questions. You then summarize the responses and look for patterns.

Vertical slices are especially useful for understanding how effectively upward and downward communication works in your new organization. You might ask, for example, "How effective was the previous manager at aligning goals in the organization?" To answer this question you could start with senior people, asking them about mission, vision, strategy, and goals, and then work your way progressively lower in the organization, asking similar questions. How far down do you need to go before people get fuzzy on how what they are doing fits into the bigger picture? People lower in the organization will not, of course, have the breadth of view of more senior staff. But they should understand their role and its relationship to mission, vision, and strategy. If they don't, it means you have work to do to establish stronger channels for downward communication.

Vertical slices likewise can be used to probe awareness of emerging challenges and opportunities as perceived on the organization's front lines. Start by talking with a selected subset of people on the front lines. This can be done individually or in small groups—for example, in informal brown-bag lunches. The key questions here concern what they see from the frontline perspective.

You then work your way up the chain, asking similar questions about challenges and opportunities. Your objective is to see whether too much filtering of information happens on the way up. Are people at lower levels seeing key developments that are not being communicated to senior levels? If so, you have to remove blocks to upward communication.

Finally, *interface triangulation* means looking at key interfaces between your organization and important outside groups and doing so from both sides. How do your "customers" perceive your organization? Does this match up with how frontline people in the organization perceive relationships with customers? If both perceive your organization as performing poorly, you have work to do. If customers are unhappy but people in your organization think everything is fine, you have even more work to do.

Horizontal slices, vertical slices, and interface triangulation are three useful examples of a broader class of structured learning methods that involve asking groups of people similar questions. The goal is to identify patterns, spot anomalies, and, later, to test hypotheses. So don't feel limited to these approaches. Think about the type of insights that would be most helpful, and design your learning methods accordingly.

Understanding Your Learning Style

Finally, as you engage in learning about your new organization, keep in mind that you have a *learning style*—a set of personal preferences developed over time about what and how you like to learn.[7] Some people prefer to learn from hard data, like reports and analyses, and others prefer to base their judgments more on expert opinion.

Some people are experiential learners—they like to dive in and learn by taking action and seeing what happens. When they buy a new piece of software, they quickly take it for a test-drive to see whether they can make it do what they need it to. Others are more conceptual in their approach, preferring to observe for a while and develop a model of what is going on. They read the manual.

To get a clearer sense of what your actual learning style is, complete the exercise in "Assessing Your Learning Style."

It's not a question of right styles and wrong styles. Whatever your style may be, it is certain to have both strengths that help accelerate and retain new learning and weaknesses that create blind spots and impede new learning. That's the bad news. The good

---

Assessing Your Learning Style

In general, do you put more stock in hard data (numbers and analyses) or soft data (expert assessments and others' observations)? (You probably rely on both, but which do you give more credence to?)

___ Hard data   ___ Soft data

In general, do you prefer to learn by diving into a situation (an experiential learning style) or by observing for a while before taking action (a conceptual learning style)? (Once again, you probably do both, but which feels most natural to you?)

___ Dive in   ___ Observe for a while

What are the implications of your learning style for potential blind spots during a transition?

_____

_____

_____

news is that styles are preferences, not destiny, and you have the scope to adjust your approach. When devising your plan for accelerated learning during a transition to a new leadership role, therefore, it is essential to recognize the strengths and weaknesses of your learning style.

If your learning style is not a good match for the situation you face, figure out how to compensate. This means disciplining yourself to act against those preferences if the situation demands you do so. It also means building teams and advice networks with people who have different, complementary learning styles.

Conclusion

Sandra Martin presents a model of leadership excellence. Stepping into a major crisis situation without much preparation and in an environment of heavy scrutiny, she demonstrated the importance of planned learning. Had she adopted a more unilateral approach, ignoring the existing staff and assuming she knew the answers, the team certainly would not have succeeded as it did.

If there is one enduring lesson to be drawn from this chapter it is this: however satisfied you may be with the final version of your learning plan, you will be changing it. Your learning agenda and strategies will inevitably shift as you learn more about your new organization and your own requirements for new knowledge. Plan to return to this chapter from time to time to reassess your learning agenda and create new learning plans.

ACCELERATION CHECKLIST

1. What is your learning agenda?

2. Do you only need to understand the technical side of the business, or is it critical that you understand culture and politics as well?

3. Based on what you know now, compose a list of questions to guide your early inquiry. If you have begun to form

hypotheses about what is going on, what are they and how will you test them?

4. Given the questions you want to answer, which individuals and group are most likely to provide you with solid actionable insights?

5. How might you increase the efficiency of your learning process? What are some ways you might extract more actionable insights for your investment of time and energy?

4

Secure Early Wins

J OE RAAB was a public-service veteran who, after six
years as a section head, had been promoted to manage a thirty-person financial operations division. In his
new role, Joe was responsible for overseeing the work of his former
section, payroll, as well as billing, accounts receivable, and dis-
bursements, responsibilities handled by the two other sections that
comprised the agency's office of financial management and were
now under his command. His predecessor in the position had been
an authoritarian, hard-nosed boss. Joe had chafed under that leadership and had his share of run-ins with his old boss over the years
about his boss's style. Joe also had heard regular gripes about his
boss from employees and peers. So when Joe was promoted, he
established changing the division's culture as his number one priority and set about designing a more participative way of accomplishing the division's goals.

Being intimately familiar with the division's work and personnel,
Joe felt free to rapidly develop and implement a more inclusive leadership strategy. He was confident he would be able to better draw on
the staff's experience, to better motivate people to seek improvements in the way the division operated, and, ultimately, to boost the
division's productivity—a necessary goal in the face of recent budget
and staff reductions. Eager to signal positive change to the division
as soon as possible, he closeted himself for several hours a day,

researching the literature on participative management styles and preparing his plan. At the end of his first month, Joe called an all-hands meeting and revealed the strategy he had developed.

The strategy had three pillars: more independence and individual accountability for performance, more flexibility for supervisors in dealing with employee performance problems, and increased supervisory participation in developing division objectives and accountability for achieving them. When Joe finished his thirty-minute presentation, he asked for questions and was taken aback by the response. Instead of the enthusiasm he expected, there was at first silence and then widely expressed skepticism that the strategy could or would work. Joe tried to ask probing questions about why there was such doubt, but the answers were evasive or vague. Frustrated, he closed the meeting and retired to his office to ponder what had happened.

What *had* happened? Though Joe disdained the constraining effects of the former authoritarian culture, he did not adequately consider the extent to which staff had adjusted to it over the years before he took over as division head. Misled by the informal griping he had heard for years, he underestimated the degree to which employees had grown used to a "do as you're told" environment, and overestimated the probability that they would immediately see the benefits of a departure from it.

Put another way, Joe thought he was leading a turnaround when arguably all that was required was a realignment. Consequently, Joe's liberating idea of more across-the-board personal accountability was seen by employees and supervisors alike as increasing personal risk, and it was frightening. Joe, despite his own experience as an insider, had assumed that everyone shared his perspective of the organization's extant culture. Now he had to fight the uphill battle of selling the concept to people he had thought would welcome it but who actually viewed the whole thing as unworkable, if not dangerous. This initial failure to get a major early win caused Joe to lose some credibility with his staff and endangered the kind of long-term improvements he wanted to be the hallmark of his tenure.

Joe Raab was correct in believing that an early win in the form of a quickly implemented departure from his predecessor's authoritarian management style would establish his credibility and signal to his new organization that favorable change was on the way. What he missed, however, was the importance of getting those early wins in the right way. Above all, a new leader wants to avoid early losses because once the tide begins running against you, it is tough to recover.

Getting Off to the Right Start

As you come to understand more about your new organization, you can begin to shift more attention to defining your goals and beginning to create some momentum. As you do so, however, you should be careful to avoid common traps into which new leaders fall:

- **Not adjusting for the culture.** While leaders coming into an organization from the outside are most at risk for this kind of trap, insiders, such as Joe, can also be affected. The outsider might assume that the culture he or she absorbed in a previous assignment is the same everywhere else, and the insider might assume that everyone in the organization perceives things the way he or she does. Either way, making untested assumptions about the culture is dangerous and can put you behind the curve during the most tenuous period of your transition.

- **Failing to focus.** It is all too easy to take on too much during a transition, and the results can be ruinous. You can end up heading off in many directions at once, confusing your bosses, subordinates, and supporters. You cannot hope to achieve results in more than a couple of areas during your transition. Thus, it is essential to identify promising opportunities and then focus relentlessly on turning them into wins.

- **Misreading the situation.** In our research we found the most common cause for transition failures among new leaders of government programs to be misreading the situation they face in their new assignments. As Joe's experience shows, what constitutes an early win will differ dramatically from one ST$_A$RS situation to another. Just getting people to talk about the organization and its challenges can be a big win in a realignment but a waste of time in a turnaround. That's why it is so important to do a careful diagnosis of the situation early on.

- **Failing to get wins that matter.** It is important to get early wins that energize your subordinates. But your boss's opinion about what counts matters too—a lot. Remember the importance of defining expectations. Even if you do not fully support your boss's priorities, it is important to make them central in calculating what kinds of early wins to aim for. Addressing the problems your boss sees as important will go a long way toward building your credibility with him or her and easing your access to resources.

- **Letting your means undermine your ends.** Process matters. If you achieve impressive results in a manner that is seen as manipulative, underhanded, or inconsistent with the prevailing culture, you are setting yourself up for trouble. So how you get your wins is as important as what they are. An early win that is accomplished in a way that exemplifies the behaviors you hope to instill in your new organization is a double win.

- **Pursuing early wins for their own sake.** There is no question that you need to get some early wins to build momentum. But the temptation is strong to do this by plucking the lowest-hanging fruit available to you. The problem with those kinds of wins is that you may succeed in creating some early momentum, only to sputter out because you haven't laid the foundation for more sustained improvements in performance. It's like trying to launch a rocket into orbit when the first stage fires but the second stage is a dud. Your efforts to get wins must, therefore, be tightly connected to the broader set of goals you are striving to accomplish, long term as well as short term. Ideally, your wins do double duty by creating momentum early on while at the same time laying the foundation for achieving longer-term goals.

Planning to Succeed

The process for establishing your goals and figuring out where and how to secure early wins is summarized in the *goal grid* illustrated in figure 4-1. The rows of the grid define the time horizon—one-year goals in the upper row and shorter-term early-win goals in the lower row. The columns of the grid differentiate between the concrete performance goals you want to achieve in the left-hand column and the supporting changes in behavior you seek to realize in the right-hand column. The numbers indicate the order in which you should undertake key tasks in your first cycle of planning.

Step #1: Define One-Year Goals

The place to begin is in the upper-left cell, which concerns the concrete performance goals you will strive to achieve by the end of your first year. The one-year deadline is somewhat arbitrary, and you should adjust it as necessary. The key is to choose a deadline that is

FIGURE 4-1

The goal grid

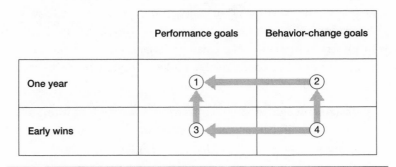

	Performance goals	Behavior-change goals
One year	①	②
Early wins	③	④

far enough out that you can achieve significant performance goals, yet not so far out that you can't realistically plan.

You need to establish one-year goals to have a concrete target that guides your efforts both to get early wins and to lay a foundation for deeper improvements in performance. Well-defined goals will pull you forward. Critically, they will help you avoid getting caught up in firefighting or in overly tactical efforts to secure early wins.

So start by focusing on what you need to achieve in a year, and answer the following questions:

- What are the top few things you need to accomplish by the end of twelve months?

- What performance metrics will you use to evaluate your progress?

- Are there intermediate goals or milestones you need to hit?

Strive to be as detailed and precise as you can about what success looks like. Of course, you should factor in what you have learned about your boss's "must-do's," as well as the expectations of key stakeholders. You also should keep the results of your ST_ARS analysis in mind. What will you commit yourself to achieving in the various elements of your portfolio?

Step #2: Identify Supporting Behavior Changes

The next step is to focus on the upper-right cell of the goal grid—changes in behavior necessary to support achievement of your one-year goals. The starting point is to assess whether people in the organization are systematically behaving in ways that will undermine your efforts to improve performance. What concrete behavioral issues do you need to confront? Examples of dysfunctional behavior patterns include:

- **Inward focus.** Too much inward focus and use of internally defined performance metrics and not enough focus on customers and benchmarking with high-performing organizations.

- **Diffuse accountability.** Decision-making processes that diffuse responsibility so much that no one is held accountable for unsatisfactory performance.

- **Internal conflict.** Ongoing conflict between groups or individuals in the organization that has sapped collective energy and impaired performance.

- **Complacency.** A mix of low standards and a long history of satisfactory performance that has drained any sense of urgency and need for improvement from the organization.

Given your diagnosis of needed behavior changes, what is your vision for how people will behave differently by the end of a year? How will you be sure that the actions you take to get improved performance don't undermine your efforts to create a high-achievement culture? Once again, strive to be as precise and detailed as you can, both about what the dysfunctional behaviors are and about how you want people to behave differently.

Step #3: Plan Early-Win Initiatives

The next step is to focus on the lower-left cell—defining the initiatives you will pursue to secure early wins. As you do this, keep in mind that early wins should both help build momentum in the short run and simultaneously lay the foundation for achieving your longer-term goals.

The best candidates for early wins are problems that you can tackle reasonably quickly with modest expenditure and that will yield visible operational and fiscal gains. Examples might be bottlenecks in work processes that act as drags on organizational productivity. Seek to identify at most two or three key areas where you will seek to achieve rapid improvement. If you take on too many initiatives, you risk losing focus. But don't put all your eggs in one basket: build a portfolio of early-win initiatives so that successes in one will balance disappointments in others.

To translate your goals into specific initiatives to secure early wins, work through the following guidelines:

- **Keep your long-term goals in mind.** The actions that you take to secure early wins should, to the greatest extent possible, also lay the foundation for achieving your one-year goals and support your efforts to change behavior.

- **Identify promising focal points.** Focal points are areas or processes where improvement can dramatically strengthen the organization's overall operation. Try to identify as many such opportunities as you can.

- **Concentrate on the most promising of these focal points.** Concentrating on a few focal points you identify will reduce the time and energy needed to achieve tangible results. Improving performance early in these areas will win you freedom and space to pursue more extensive changes.

- **Launch early-win projects.** Design initiatives targeted at your chosen focal points that you can undertake right away. Successful early projects set your overall plan in motion, energize your staff, and yield real improvements that can be reported to your boss.

- **Elevate change agents.** Identify the people in your organization, at all levels, who have the insight, drive, and incentives to advance your agenda. Provide them with leadership roles and reward them for their successes.

As you plan to get your early wins, keep in mind that what constitutes a win varies considerably among the different ST$_A$Rs situations. In a start-up situation success in developing a coherent strategy for what the organization will seek to do and, critically, not seek to do is an early win. In a turnaround situation your simple arrival, especially if you have already built a reputation for effectiveness, can be an early win, as can early actions to stabilize the situation and put a plan in place. (This was borne out of our research. Several of the executives we interviewed stated that when brought into new leadership positions in the aftermath of an organizational performance failure, their just being there constituted an early win in the sense that they either successfully competed for the position or were personally chosen to improve the organization's performance. Either way, they felt that they walked through the door with credibility.) In a realignment situation your arrival is not an early win, but success in raising awareness of the need for change most certainly is. In a sustaining-success situation simply taking the time to learn about what has made the organization successful, and communicating that you have learned and can be trusted to make good decisions, can be a big early win.

Step #4: Use Early Wins to Drive Behavior Change

The final step concerns the lower-right cell of the matrix—pursuing early wins in ways that help establish new models of behavior in your organization, and so help you to achieve your one-year behavior-change goals. Note that there are two arrows linking this cell to its neighbors. This highlights the need to set up projects in ways that both drive your early-win initiatives and simultaneously advance your longer-terms behavior-change objectives.

The ways you go about getting early wins—in terms of how you pursue them and how you get the necessary support of others where needed—are valuable tools for beginning to establish new behaviors in your organization. And changing behaviors is an essential first step in changing dysfunctional aspects of organizational culture. You should therefore strive, to the maximum extent possible, to leverage your efforts to secure early wins to introduce new behaviors. If you are seeking to improve the performance of a key process in your organization, for example, you might consider forming a process-improvement team and adopting a rigorous process-improvement methodology. By doing this, you can begin to instill a new discipline in the organization while simultaneously providing an action-learning experience in which people learn to use new tools. And you can thus establish a template for follow-on process-improvement efforts for future learning.

More generally, you should think of your early-win initiatives as projects, and apply rigorous project-planning methods to pursue

them. The following checklist summarizes a set of planning guidelines that you can use to help you organize each major initiative you
decide to pursue. To plan each early-win project, create a worksheet
that answers these questions:

- **Focus.** What is the focal point for this project? What are the
  concrete goals and time lines?

- **Oversight.** How will you oversee this project? Who else
  should participate in oversight to help get buy-in for implementing results?

- **Goals.** What are the goals, intermediate milestones, and
  time frames for achieving both? Who will be responsible for
  the various pieces of the overall project?

- **Leadership.** Who will lead the project? What training, if any,
  do they need to be successful?

- **Abilities.** What mix of skills and representation should be
  included? Who needs to be included because of their skills
  and knowledge? Who needs to be included because they represent important constituencies?

- **Means.** What additional resources—for example, facilita-
  tion—does the team need to be successful?

- **Process.** Are there change models or structured processes
  you want team members to use? If so, how will they become
  familiar with the approach? How will you ensure that they
  employ it in a disciplined manner?

As you do this planning, keep in mind that your choice of behavior-
change techniques should be a function of your group's structure,
processes, skills, and—above all—situation. Consider the difference
between promoting behavior change in turnaround and realignment
situations. In a turnaround you face a combination of time pressure
and the need to rapidly identify and secure the organization's core
mission. Techniques such as bringing in new people and setting up
project teams to pursue specific performance-improvement initiatives

often are a good fit. In realignments, however, you should start out with less obvious approaches to behavior change. By resetting performance measures and starting benchmarking, for example, you set the stage for collective visioning about how to realign the business.

Finally, keep in mind your overall goal: creating a virtuous cycle that reinforces wanted behavior and helps you achieve your longer-terms performance-improvement objectives. Remember that you are aiming at relatively modest early wins as a basis for pursuing more fundamental changes later.

Connecting with Your Organization

Completing the goal-grid process will help you identify concrete opportunities to secure early wins that have a measurable impact on performance. But you can't really do this planning until you have climbed up the learning curve to a substantial degree. You can, however, still secure some wins very early in your tenure. Even as you undertake the effort to learn and plan, you should keep your eyes open for opportunities to score small victories and to send signals that things are changing. Such small victories will help you build personal credibility and, in turn, give you more scope to pursue your early-win initiatives.

It is often said that you only get one chance at making a good first impression. Because your earliest actions will have a disproportionate effect on how you are perceived, think through how you will get connected to your new organization. Remember the experience of Joe Raab—even if you are an insider who has been promoted, your connection to the organization has changed because of your new status and must be reassessed. What messages do you want to get across about who you are and what you represent? What are the best ways to convey those messages? Identify your key audiences—direct reports, other employees, key external constituencies—and craft a few messages tailored to each. These messages need not be about what you plan to do; that would be premature. They should focus instead on who you are, the values and goals you represent, your style, and how you like to manage teams.

Think too about modes of engagement. How will you introduce yourself in your new role? Should your first meetings with direct reports be as a group or one-on-one? Will they be informal get-acquainted meetings or task focused? If your organization has facilities in other locations, how will you handle those meetings—will you go there or invite the field people to your office?

As you make progress in getting connected, identify and act as quickly as you can to remove minor irritants in your organization. If there are previously strained external relations, focus on repairing them. Cut out redundant meetings, shorten excessively long ones, and improve physical space problems. All this helps build your credibility early on.

When you arrive, people will rapidly begin to assess you and your capabilities. Your credibility, or lack of it, will depend on how people in the organization would answer the following questions about you:

- Do you display the insight and steadiness to make tough decisions?

- Do you display values that people relate to, admire, and want to emulate?

- Are you energetic?

- Do you insist on high levels of performance from yourself and others?

Fairly or not, people in the organization will begin to form opinions based on little data. Your early actions, good and bad, will shape perceptions. Once opinion about you has begun to harden, it will be difficult to change. And the opinion-forming process happens remarkably quickly. So how do you build personal credibility? In part, it is about marketing yourself effectively. You want people to associate you with attractive qualities. There is no single right answer for how to do this. In general, however, new leaders are perceived as credible when they are:

- **Demanding but able to be satisfied.** Effective leaders press people to make realistic commitments and then hold those people to their promises. But if you are never satisfied, you'll just sap people's motivation.

- **Accessible but not too familiar.** Being accessible does not mean making yourself available indiscriminately. It means being approachable—in a way that preserves your authority.

- **Decisive but judicious.** New leaders communicate their capacity to take charge without jumping too quickly into decisions that they are not ready for. Early in your transition, you want to project decisiveness but defer important decisions until you know enough to make them.

- **Focused but flexible.** Avoid setting up a vicious cycle and alienating others by coming across as rigid and unwilling to consider multiple solutions to a problem. Effective new leaders establish authority by zeroing in on issues, consulting others, and encouraging input.

- **Active without causing commotion.** There is a fine line between creating momentum and overwhelming your employees. Make things happen without pushing people into the burnout zone.

- **Willing to make tough calls but humane.** You may have to make some tough calls early on, especially if you find yourself dealing with budget or staff reductions. Effective new leaders do what is needed, but they do it in ways that preserve people's dignity and that are perceived by others as fair.

Then there is the power of stories in your efforts to build credibility. Leaders' early actions often generate potent stories that define them either as heroes or villains. To nudge the mythology in a positive direction, look for and leverage *teachable moments*. These are actions that clearly display what you are about; they also model the kinds of behavior you want to encourage. They need not be dramatic statements or confrontations. A teachable moment can be as simple, and as hard, as asking the penetrating question that crystallizes your group's understanding of some key problem.

Leading Change

Although in most government agencies dramatic change often is inhibited by myriad statutes, regulations, and otherwise mandated constraints, constructive change is entirely possible, as evidenced by the many examples of outstanding leadership by public-sector executives who improved the delivery and quality of the public services their agencies provided. So as you approach the task of planning for and achieving important early wins, it is vital that you have a clear sense of what strategy holds the best chance of success, keeping two distinctions in mind: planned change versus collective learning and attitude change versus behavior change.

Planned Change Versus Collective Learning

Once you have identified the most important problems or issues you need to address, the next step is to decide whether to engage in a plan-then-implement change strategy or in the promotion of collective learning as a means of stimulating awareness of the problems to be addressed.[1] The straightforward plan-then-implement approach to change works well when you are sure that you have the following five supporting planks:

1. **Awareness.** A critical mass of people is aware of the need for change.

2. **Consensus.** You and other key players understand what needs to be changed and why.

3. **Vision.** You have a compelling vision and a solid strategy.

4. **Plan.** You have the expertise to put together a detailed plan.

5. **Support.** You have a sufficiently powerful coalition to support implementation.

The plan-then-implement approach to change might work well in turnaround situations; for example, where people accept there is a problem, the fixes are more technical than cultural or political, and people are hungry for a solution. If any of these five conditions are not met, however, the pure plan-to-implement approach to change can be a trap. If you are facing a realignment, for example, and people are in denial or otherwise resistant to the need for, practical value of, or potential benefits of change, your plan, like Joe Raab's, will likely be greeted with skepticism. You may, therefore, need to build awareness of the need for change, to sharpen the diagnosis of the problem, to fashion a more compelling vision and strategy, or to create a stronger coalition of supporters.

To accomplish any of these goals, you should focus on setting up a collective-learning process, and not on developing and imposing plans for change. If many people in the organization are willfully blind to emerging problems, for example, you have to initiate a process for overcoming their resistance. Rather than mounting a frontal assault, however, you should engage in a more subtle approach, aiming to raise their awareness of the organization's problems and of the consequent need for change.

A collective-learning approach may include exposing key people to new ways of operating and thinking about your agency's mission. Or you can benchmark other highly successful organizations. Or you can engage your staff in an off-site brainstorming session about primary objectives or about ways to improve existing work processes.

The key, then, is to figure out which parts of the change process is best addressed through planning and which are better dealt with through collective learning. Use the chart in figure 4-2 as a guide for thinking about how you should best approach a change you want to make in your organization.

Attitude Change Versus Behavior Change

As you plan to get early wins, remember that the means you use are as important as the ends you achieve. The initiatives you put in place to get early wins should do double duty by establishing new standards of behavior. To change your organization, you will most likely have to change parts of its culture.

FIGURE 4-2

Diagnosing approaches to leading change

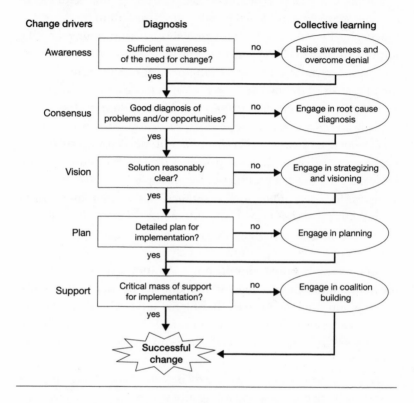

Cultural change is a difficult undertaking. Your organization may have well-ingrained bad habits that you need to break, and we know how difficult it is for one person to change his or her own habitual patterns in any significant way, never mind changing the habits of a mutually reinforcing collection of people. In the recent past, government executives, as well as their private-sector counterparts, have had to address this problem in order to remove barriers to the development and advancement of minorities and women, to accommodate environmental and work-safety advancements, and many other at the time controversial and difficult-to-implement imperatives. In the course of succeeding, they learned a valuable lesson: simply blowing up the existing culture and starting over is rarely, if ever, the right answer.

People—and organizations—have limits on the amount of change they can absorb all at once. And organizational cultures have virtues as well as flaws; they provide predictability and can be sources of pride. If you send the message that there is nothing good about the existing organization and its culture, you will take away from people a key source of stability in times of change. You also will deprive yourself of a wellspring of energy into which you could tap to improve performance.

The key is to identify both the good and the bad elements of the existing culture. Elevate and reward the good even as you seek to eliminate the bad. These functional aspects of the familiar culture are a bridge that can help carry people from the past to the future.

Making Waves

Finally, as you plan for your transition and beyond, think in terms of what John Gabarro described as successive *waves of change,* as illustrated in figure 4-3.[2] The figure charts the intensity of change a

FIGURE 4-3

Waves of change

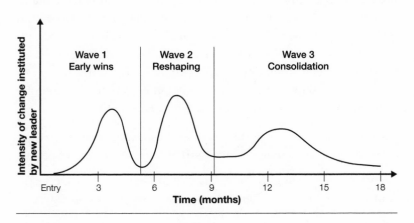

leader institutes over time. What you see are a series of waves. Each wave consists of efforts to (1) learn about the organization, (2) plan changes, (3) implement plans, and (4) observe and learn from the results. The reductions in the intensity of change are important both to give you the opportunity to figure out what has and has not worked (it's hard to learn if you continue to make changes) and to give people a chance to catch their breath and celebrate success.

In the first wave, you learn, plan, implement, and observe to secure early wins. As discussed earlier in the chapter, you tailor your early initiatives to build personal credibility, establish key relationships, and take advantage of the high-potential opportunities for short-term improvements in organizational performance. Done well, this helps you build momentum and deepen your knowledge.

The first phase sets the stage for deeper learning and potentially more far-reaching change in Wave 2. Often this wave addresses more fundamental issues of strategy, structure, systems, and skills to reshape the organization. This is when real gains in organizational performance are achieved. But you will not get these gains if you do not first secure early wins in the first wave.

If you are successful and if the organization's environment remains stable, you may have the luxury of consolidating your efforts in Wave 3. If not, you may need to undertake a more fundamental wave of change.

It is important to understand, however, that the patterns of change differ radically with each ST_ARS situation. In the more time-critical situations—start-ups and turnarounds—you should expect to begin your first wave earlier. The intensity of change, as perceived by people in the organization, also will be greater. In realignment and sustaining-success situations, by contrast, you can afford to take more time to learn and plan before undertaking the first wave—a lesson Joe Raab might have benefited from.

Conclusion

Early wins are among the most important elements of a successful transition, for without them you will have lost the opportunity to gain crucial personal credibility and lay the foundation for longer-term success. But as important as early wins are, they are not enough by themselves to assure the achievement of your longer-term performance improvement and behavior change. They must be viewed as a critical first step into the future, and answering the following questions in the acceleration checklist will help assure you that you are off to the best start.

ACCELERATION CHECKLIST

1. What are your longer-term performance-improvement and behavior-change priorities, and how does what you are doing during your transition relate to them?

2. What are the most promising focal points for your early performance-improvement efforts?

3. Given what you need to do, what resources are absolutely essential? With fewer resources, what would you have to forgo? What would the benefits of more resources be?

4. What can you do during your transition to begin to change behaviors constructively?

5. Given the changes you wish to make, in what areas do you need to undertake collective learning, and in what areas can you rely on a plan-to-implement approach?

6. Given your ST_ARS situation, what should be the timing and extent of the waves of change you will implement?

5

Build the Team

JULIE DAVIS had risen rapidly through her agency's ranks as a procurement specialist, earning a reputation for self-direction and reliable handling of complex assignments with minimum supervision along the way. Then she was promoted to lead a new procurement organization—one that had been formed from the consolidation of two former sections and was a result of budget reductions and a recent reorganization. The sections were staffed by a mixture of clerical and administrative employees, as well as contract-administration specialists who directly oversaw the performance of the agency's various contractors and were empowered to authorize payment when work was completed. Julie's responsibilities included complex IT and construction procurements for her agency, tasks she was well familiar with, but added to those was the direct supervision of ten newly assigned employees. It was Julie's first supervisory assignment, and she approached it eagerly.

Julie had thrived in an environment of hands-off supervision and had become wary of the kind of micromanagement she had heard a number of peers complain about. She therefore decided that a light-handed management style would be the approach she would take with her new staff. She would spell out work priorities, set objectives, and allocate resources, but beyond that she believed individual staff members would be better motivated if left consider-able discretion about how to carry out their assigned tasks.

After six months, Julie was surprised to learn via a 360-degree performance evaluation that, though her supervisors and her peers praised her performance, some contractors and key internal cus-tomers were reporting problematic service and many on her new staff criticized her for being indifferent to their work problems. While a few staff members enjoyed the autonomy they were given, the lack of supervision caused the majority to become risk averse. The result? Important contract-administration problems often were not addressed because staff members were uncertain of the direc-tion they should take and felt uncomfortable about seeking guid-ance from their new supervisor. Furthermore, when Julie endeavored to trace the sources of customer complaints, she found that her hands-off approach left her unable to evaluate employees ade-quately. As a result, she could not tell whether the complaints were due to poor employee performance or to inadequate employee training and direction.

After hearing all this, Julie astutely decided to make a midcourse correction in the way she was leading. Her well-intended avoidance of micromanagement was not being seen as a benefit by most staff members and, she feared, could be contributing to customer dissatis-faction. So she began looking at her team-building responsibilities in a new light. As a first move, she met with each staff member to discuss the feedback she had received, assuring him or her that she under-stood and accepted it, and to ask about some ideas for improvement.

She then scheduled a one-day off-site meeting to review the organization's performance over the past six months, to identify successes and problem areas, to set performance objectives for the next six months, and to develop an agreed-upon approach to achieving those objectives. This session not only resulted in clari-fied group and individual performance objectives, but it also en-abled Julie to witness firsthand the group's dynamics and better evaluate the individuals involved.

Once back at work, Julie began a series of development-planning sessions with each staff member to discuss his or her training requirements in the context of the new six-month plan and the employee's longer-term career aspirations. Julie considered revising who did what work, but she wisely decided to give the staff more time to develop under her new approach before making dramatic changes to the structure.

At the end of the next six months, Julie's 360-degree evaluation had changed. No contractors or customers had complained. In fact, several of them complimented the improvements in responsiveness they had experienced over the past six months. Moreover, Julie's staff support was solid.

Fortunately, Julie was astute enough to see that her initial leadership approach was having an effect opposite to the one she sought, and she took quick action to turn the situation from a problem to a success story. Less capable leaders, however, might have become defensive and, by blaming the staff for not responding in the "right" way, made the situation worse. When Julie chose instead to make a midcourse correction to her leadership style, one that focused more attention on her staff, she not only demonstrated her acumen as a leader, but she also brought about rapid improvements in her group's performance and in her standing as a credible and trustworthy leader.

Repairing the Airplane in Midflight

In most government situations, even if they are start-ups, there are constraints on a new leader's ability to staff the organization as he or she might prefer at the start. These constraints come in the form of a predetermined budget and personnel allocations, transfers and hires who have high job security and were assigned before a new leader took over, and maybe even labor-management agreements that affect staffing patterns and work processes. Therefore, most new public managers like Julie make do, at least for a while, with the set of people they inherit. Nevertheless, they must not overlook, as Julie did at first, the critical importance of team building.

Building a team in a governmental context is a major transition challenge that can be compared to repairing an airplane in midflight.

The plane (i.e., the existing team) is already in flight when you arrive, and you have to be careful that you don't make too many changes too early. After all, there is work that needs to be done, and team members, even those who are relatively weak, will likely have the critical knowledge necessary to keep the plane in the air. So you have to be careful not to try and change too much too fast, lest you precipitate a crash.

At the same time, it's easy to conclude that there is nothing much you can do to reshape the team you have inherited. Doing so, however, is a big mistake because people are the most important resource you have to get things done. A weak team inevitably translates into either poor performance or places an intolerable burden on you to pick up the slack and keep things moving. Admittedly, it is difficult to make changes in your team; this is another area where managers in the public sector face more constraints in leading change than their cousins in business. But it's not impossible to move out really poor performers; it just takes patience and time.

To build your team, begin by assessing it. A thorough evaluation of your existing team provides the necessary foundation for planning how you will restructure it. This evaluation, in turn, will help you assess the potential to make productive changes in goals, measures, and rewards within the boundaries inevitably imposed by existing rules. In parallel with this, you can evaluate and make changes to key team processes—for example, those concerning information sharing and decision making. Of course, good processes can't turn sow's ears into silk purses, but they can help you compensate for weaker performers and leverage the strengths of your stronger players. By instituting a stronger system of performance management, for example, Julie was able to significantly improve her staff's performance.

Assessing Your New Team

Whenever you assume a new leadership position in an organization, you are likely to inherit some good performers, some average ones, and some who need significant improvement. You also will inherit a group with its own internal dynamics and politics—indeed, some members may even have hoped to be selected for the job you now hold. During your first few months, therefore, it is important to sort out who is who, what roles each individual plays, and how the group has worked in the past.

Establishing Your Evaluative Criteria

Inevitably, you will find yourself forming impressions of team members as you meet them. These early impressions are important, but do not let them hold you hostage. A more rigorous evaluation will be needed before final determinations can be made about individual performance and potential.

To assess your team in a thorough and even-handed way, establish the evaluative criteria you will use. On what basis will you evaluate the people on your team? What attributes will be more and less valuable? Few new leaders are consciously aware of the criteria they use. This creates potential vulnerabilities because, as we will discuss later, your criteria should depend on the situation you are facing.

Start by considering these criteria:

- **Competence.** Does this person have the necessary technical competence and experience to do the job?

- **Judgment.** Does this person exercise good judgment when faced with time pressures or when information is ambiguous?

- **Energy.** Does this team member approach his or her tasks enthusiastically or lethargically?

- **Focus.** Is this person capable of setting or adhering to priorities, or is he or she prone to divergence?

- **Relationships.** Does this person get along with other team members and support collective decisions, or is he or she difficult to work with?

- **Trust.** Can you rely on this person to keep his or her word and follow through on commitments?

To get a quick read on the criteria you use, complete table 5-1. Allow yourself 100 points to divide among the six criteria according to the *relative weight* you place on them when you evaluate direct reports. Record those numbers in the middle column, making sure they add up to 100. Now identify one of these as your *threshold criterion*. If a person does not meet a basic threshold on that dimension, nothing else matters. Label your threshold issue with an asterisk in the right-hand column.

Now take a step back. Does this accurately represent the values you wish to apply when you evaluate members of your team? If so, does this analysis suggest any potential blind spots in the way you evaluate people? Your selection of your threshold criterion is critical, as we will discuss further later, and should be done with care.

Your assessments are likely to contain certain assumptions about what you can and cannot change about the people who work for you. For instance, if you score relationships low and judgment high, you may think that relationships within your team are something you can influence, whereas you cannot influence someone's capacity for judgment. Likewise, you may have designated trust as a

TABLE 5-1

Ranking evaluative criteria

Evaluative criteria	Relative weights (Divide 100 points among the six issues)	Threshold issue (Designate one issue with an asterisk)
Competence		
Judgment		
Energy		
Focus		
Relationships		
Trust		
	Total = 100 points	

threshold issue—many leaders do—because you believe that you must be able to trust those who report to you, and because you believe that trustworthiness is a trait that cannot be changed.

How would this exercise have helped Julie avoid that early warning about the weaknesses in her chosen leadership strategy? She could have gotten a quick reading on whether her new staff members were positioned to perform well independently, as her hands-off approach assumed, or whether they required more structure and direction during the first phase of the transition to the new organization and a new leader. Furthermore, she would have got early insight into who among her staff were likely to be problem performers and compensated for it by reallocating the workload, assigning the more critical work to the employees who seemed most likely to perform well under her system of leadership. In this way, contractor and customer dissatisfaction could have been avoided during the transition phase.

Factoring In the Situation

To what extent should your evaluation criteria vary depending on the nature of the ST_ARS situation you are facing? Potentially, a lot. In a sustaining-success situation, for example, you may have time to develop one or two high-potential members of your team. In a turnaround, by contrast, you will need people who can perform at a high level right away. Likewise, in a start-up you may be willing to trade off some trust for a higher level of energy and focus. In a realignment you will need people who recognize that changes need to be made, just not necessarily at the speed demanded in a turnaround. It is worthwhile to spend some time thinking about the criteria you will use to evaluate your new team. Having done so, you will be better prepared to make a rigorous and systematic evaluation.

Julie Davis missed an early opportunity to understand that she was facing a mixture of realignment and sustaining-success situations. If she had taken the time to do some assessments of her new staff before deciding on a leadership strategy, she would have been in a better position to understand the staff's requirements and invested more time communicating her vision for change while still maintaining a high level of customer service.

Making Individual Assessments

After arming yourself with deeper insight into the criteria you will use, you should make individual assessments of your direct reports. The first test is whether an employee fails to meet your threshold requirement. This is why your identification of the threshold criterion counts for so much in your evaluation process. For example, if you rated technical competence as your threshold requirement, you should carefully review such measures as error rates and consult with your customers as to which, if any, team member's work often must be returned or amended because of technical omissions or mistakes. If relationships are your threshold requirement, carefully observe who in your group meetings is supportive of others and who may be unduly competitive or self-serving.

For people who meet your threshold requirement, you need to take the next step and assess relative strengths and weaknesses. If you are managing a team whose members have diverse functional expertise—such as a collection of administrative support functions, or a group responsible for research as well as engineering work—you will need to get a handle on their competence in their respective areas. This can be difficult, especially for first-time managers. If you came to your position from the inside, try to solicit the opinions of people you respect and trust in each function who know the individuals on your team.

If you are entering a general management role, consider developing your own template for each of the functions. A good template consists of guidelines and warning signs for evaluating people in functions such as finance, HR, procurement, and security. To develop each template, talk to experienced managers about what they look for in these functions.

How do you go about making these assessments? Start by meeting one-on-one with each member of your new team. These meetings may take the form of informal discussions, formal performance reviews,

or a combination of both, but your own preparation and focus should
be consistent, following these four steps:

1. **Prepare for each meeting.** Familiarize yourself with each
   person's technical or professional skills so you can assess
   how he or she functions on the team. Review available personnel history, performance data, and past appraisals.
   Where appropriate, consult with customers and others who
   have had firsthand experience with the individual's work.

2. **Foster dialogue.** Too many performance interviews turn
   out to be monologues from the supervisor. These interviews
   should be planned around standardized questions, such as:

   - What do you think of our group's current level of
     performance?

   - What are the biggest challenges and opportunities facing
     us in the near term? In the long term?

   - What resources could help us do our work better?

   - How could we improve the way the team works together?

   - If you were in my position, what would you pay attention
     to *most*?

3. **Watch for verbal and nonverbal clues.** Note word choices,
   body language, and sensitive topics:

   - Notice what the individual does not say. Does the person
     volunteer information, or do you have to extract it? Does
     the person take responsibility for problems in his or her
     area? Make excuses? Blame others?

   - How consistent are the individual's facial expressions and
     body language with his or her words?

   - What topics elicit strong emotional responses? (These hot
     buttons provide clues to what motivates the individual and
     what kinds of changes he or she would be energized by.)

   - Outside of these one-on-one meetings, notice how the
     individual relates to other team members. Do relations

with other team members appear cordial and productive?
Tense and competitive? Judgmental or reserved?

4. **Test their judgment.** Keep in mind that some very bright
people have poor judgment, and some people of satisfactory competence have extraordinary judgment. It is essential to be clear about the mix of knowledge and judgment
you need from key people. The best way to assess judgment
is to work with a person for a while and observe whether he
or she is able to make sound predictions and develop good
strategies for avoiding problems. Both those abilities draw
on an individual's *mental models,* or ways of identifying the
essential features and dynamics of emerging situations and
translating those insights into effective action, which are
what judgment is all about.

As you make these assessments, discipline yourself to take notes
and record impressions after your meetings. Eventually you should
be able to fill out table 5-2 for each of your direct reports.

Assessing the Team as a Whole

Besides evaluating individual team members, assess how the entire group works. Use these techniques for spotting problems in
the team's overall dynamics:

- **Study the data.** Read reports and team meeting minutes, if
  available. If your organization conducts regular climate or
  morale surveys of individual units, examine them as well.

- **Systematically ask questions.** Assess individual responses to
  the common set of questions you asked when you met with
  individual team members. Are their answers overly uniform?
  If so, this may suggest an agreed-upon party line, but it could
  also mean that everyone shares the same impression of what
  is going on. Do the responses show little consistency? If so,
  the team may lack coherence. It is up to you to evaluate what
  you observe.

TABLE 5-2

Individual evaluations

Name:

Evaluative criteria	Importance of criteria	Strengths	Weaknesses	Confidence in assessment
Energy: Is this person a source of the right kind of energy?				
Expertise: Is this person a superior representative of his or her function?				
Match to situation: Will this person be effective in the business situation(s) that you are confronting?				
Teamwork: Will this person be an effective member of the team as a whole?				
	Total = 100			

Additional comments:

- **Probe group dynamics.** Observe how the group interacts in your early meetings. Do you detect any alliances? Particular attitudes? Leadership roles? Who tends to defer to whom on certain topics? When a particular person is speaking, do others indicate attention, disagreement, or frustration? Pay attention to these signs to test your early insights and to detect coalitions and conflicts.

Though this approach might not have been much help to Julie at the start because her team was newly formed, she correctly undertook the task at the six-month point by scheduling the off-site planning session. The intensity of such meetings and the contentiousness of some of the issues discussed among team members can provide an excellent opportunity for a new leader to discern political and cultural indicators and to integrate those indicators into a strategy for performance improvements.

Restructuring Your Team

Once your evaluations of each individual are completed, you will be equipped to make decisions about what changes you will seek to make in your team. This will, as discussed previously, depend also on the situation you are facing.

Your goal is to assign people to one of the following categories:

- **Keep in place.** The person is performing well in his or her current job.

- **Keep and develop.** The individual needs more training and development.

- **Reassign.** The person is a strong performer but is not in a position that makes the most of his or her skills or personal qualities.

- **Observe for a period.** The person requires further evaluation and needs a personal development plan.

- **Replace—high priority.** As soon as the opportunity arises, the person should be replaced.

- **Replace—low priority.** This person should be replaced, but you can afford to wait.

Use table 5-3 to summarize your conclusions about your direct reports.

After completing your summary of evaluations, you should have a clear sense of who within your group has the potential to move up. It may be tempting to move swiftly on these insights, but take care to move deliberately. Your initial impressions are likely to evolve, and those whom you deem high performers today might stumble upon further testing and experience. Similarly, those whom you assessed as having lower potential may pleasantly surprise you as you undertake to implement new policies or approaches to the work at hand. Also, promotions that result from these evaluations must always be handled deftly; moving from being a peer to holding a more senior position is one of the hardest transitions of all, regardless of level. The key is for you to take performance evaluations seriously, which means giving your first impressions a chance to prove out in actual

TABLE 5-3

Summary of evaluations

Team member	Keep in place (high performing)	Keep in place (high potential)	Keep but move	Replace (high priority)	Replace (low priority)

performance before making personnel moves that, especially in government, are most difficult to reverse if they don't work out.

You also may be tempted to try to replace low-performing people right away. But take the time to consider alternatives, as Julie wisely did. Replacing people probably is not an immediate option in many government organizations in any case, and, even if it is, if not done right it can demoralize the new team and damage your credibility.

Instead, due to the terms of various civil service regulations and labor-management agreements, it will more than likely be necessary to undertake formal remedial training efforts designed to bring the individual's performance up to satisfactory levels. This will be a time-consuming effort, but, when successful, it will improve the performance of your entire team and build your credibility as an engaged and trustworthy leader.

Even if you do not face these constraints, removing an employee can be a difficult and time-consuming process that can take many months (see "Managing Poor Performers Out of the Organization"). If there is an inadequate paper trail documenting the person's poor performance, it may take even longer. Fortunately, there are alternatives to outright termination, such as:

- **Lateral reassignments within the team.** Shift the person to another position that better suits his or her skills. While there often are regulatory conditions to lateral reassignments within a team, they can help you work through the short-term problem of having a poor performer in a key position.

- **Lateral reassignments elsewhere in the organization.** Work with your human resource office to help the person find a more suitable position in the larger organization. Sometimes, when done right, this kind of reassignment can benefit all concerned. However, do not pursue this alternative unless you believe the person can perform well in the new assignment. Simply shifting a problem performer onto someone else will damage your credibility as well as your ability to work with your peers on future problems.

Managing Poor Performers Out of the Organization

Contrary to popular belief, dismissing government employees who are chronically poor performers or who engage in egregious activities is entirely possible—*when it's done right.* But all too often supervisors and others in positions of authority, because of poor training or because they seek to avoid the conflict and onerous record keeping required, give employees who should be disciplined or removed a free pass to continue on with their counterproductive work practices. A common problem faced by many executives is receiving a recommendation for dismissal or reassignment of an employee due to poor performance when the employee has received satisfactory performance evaluations year after year. Supervisors and managers must be properly trained in conducting true, rather than perfunctory, performance evaluations and then—importantly—be supported by more senior-level executives during the ensuing appeals process, which most public-sector employees have access to either through civil service rules or union agreements. Julie Davis found herself facing such a problem while trying to trace the source of mounting customer complaints because her hands-off style left her in a position of not really knowing each member of her staff. So here are a few basic rules to follow so that you will be on solid ground when disciplinary action is required:

- Take performance evaluations seriously. It might seem easier to simply give satisfactory ratings to everyone to avoid conflict that could disrupt your organization's performance, but accepting poor performance from one employee is bound to lead to resentment from others who are working up to expectations, and will undermine your credibility.

- Make sure that everyone understands your expectations regarding job performance. Failure to specify them in a written performance plan, including training needs, will leave you in a weak position in the event that disciplinary actions are required.

- Initiate regular (at least quarterly) performance discussions with each employee that cover in specific terms his or her successes and shortcomings against the performance plan, and document the results. Give the employee a copy.

- Be acutely mindful of equal employment implications. The reality or even the appearance of impropriety in this area can lead to significant legal and morale problems for your entire agency.

- When you decide that disciplinary action is needed, make sure you keep in close contact with your human resource department, equal employment office, and legal counsel to assure all rules and laws are being followed. Nothing will undermine your credibility as a leader more quickly than having a disciplinary action reversed on appeal because of a procedural flaw.

Keep in mind that you need to keep the team performing well while at the same time you work to get the team you need to achieve your performance goals. You may therefore need to keep a disgruntled employee, a destructively competitive employee, an underperformer, or other problematic team member on the job while engineering a way to find and bring on board a replacement. (One leader we interviewed made it a point to hold off on shifting out of an organization people whose knowledge she could leverage during her transition.) Discreetly look for a successor by evaluating other team members or people from elsewhere in the organization and seeing who has the potential to move up. Be sure to work closely with your HR department, however; reassignments can be considered disciplinary actions or might have ramifications from your equal employment office if not handled properly. You do not want to enter this minefield without expert guidance.

During every phase of the team-restructuring process, take pains to treat everyone with respect. Even if people in your unit agree that a particular person should be replaced, your reputation will suffer if your actions are viewed as unfair. Do whatever you can to communicate the seriousness and care you are giving to the process of assessing each individual's capabilities and evaluating training and development needs. The people who work for you will form lasting impressions of your leadership abilities based on how you manage this part of your job.

Aligning Goals, Measures, and Rewards

Having the right people in the right jobs is essential, but it is not enough. To achieve your highest priorities and secure some early wins, you will need to define how each team member can best support your key goals. This process calls for breaking down the larger mission, goals, and strategy into their component pieces, working to assign team members responsibility for particular elements, and making each individual accountable for managing his or her goals. How do you encourage accountability? Through clear and effective design of performance metrics and incentives.

After Julie Davis received early warning signs that her light-handed style was not getting the results she was seeking, she took some strategic steps—quickly meeting with employees to assure them that their feedback was heard, scheduling an off-site planning meeting to discuss the group's performance problems and to establish goals, and then following up with individual meetings to set personal development plans. These moves corrected the misalignment of goals and measurements that were set up early on.

Defining Performance Metrics

In government agencies at all levels, macro performance criteria may be defined by statute, regulation, or centralized administrative authorities. Public-sector managers often are responsible for meeting those criteria, without having the necessary authority to marshal the resources and other tools needed to accomplish them.

While this scenario is especially true at the senior-most levels of governmental organizations, it is also a condition found in middle-management ranks. It does little good, for example, for a new manager of a procurement activity, such as Julie Davis, to insist on reducing the time it takes to award a contract when government-wide regulations specify mandatory time requirements and bidder appeal rights that slow the process. Likewise, the director of a social service agency can do very little to improve efficiency and quality in handling an increasing caseload when the legislature reduces budgets across the board without regard for how workloads will be affected. Similar examples abound throughout the public sector and often make creating specific performance criteria at the agency level a difficult task.

Still, setting exacting performance measurements of individual effort is not impossible. Though macro level goals may be predefined, agency managers at all levels still have micro level influence over individual and small-group performance. In our research we encountered many examples of leaders at the local, state, and federal levels who, though constrained by governmentwide policies, devised methods for translating general mandates into specific, measurable goals for their subordinate managers to use in developing internal performance metrics. As a rule, this was done by allotting the time to consult with people throughout the organization and gaining an understanding of organizational strengths and weaknesses before setting performance goals.

The existence of overlying constraints on resources and flexibility makes designing meaningful performance metrics a challenge, but it's one that can be met with the approaches discussed in previous chapters. Establishing and sticking to clear and explicit individual performance metrics is the best way to encourage accountability. That is, whenever possible, a manager should follow Julie Davis's example and set performance measures that will let him or her know unambiguously whether a team member has achieved the assigned goals. In doing so, avoid generally defined goals, such as "improve productivity" or "reduce expenditures." Instead, set specific targets for improvements measured in percentages or actual dollars.

Designing Incentives Systems

Any system for motivating people will consist of a blend of push and pull tools, as illustrated in figure 5-1. Generally, *push tools* are

FIGURE 5-1

Push and pull tools

Push tools align effort through authority, fear, and reward. Pull tools align effort through inspiration. To use pull tools, leaders must have very strong visioning and communication skills.

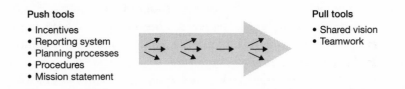

Push tools
- Incentives
- Reporting system
- Planning processes
- Procedures
- Mission statement

Pull tools
- Shared vision
- Teamwork

things like financial compensation and awards plans, performance-measurement systems, and budget increases for success in attaining a goal that motivate people mainly through the fear of the consequences of failure or the promise of financial reward for success. *Pull tools,* such as a compelling and widely shared vision, a culture that recognizes success, potential for professional development and advancement, and a motivated and engaged team inspire people by invoking a positive and exciting image of the future.

One of the starkest areas of contrast between the public and private sectors is the nature and motivating power of financial performance incentives. In business this issue tends to be a relatively straightforward matter of sharing in the financial benefits derived from a successful business plan. In government, however, using financial incentives as a way of promoting improved individual or group performance is notably more complicated for a number of reasons.

First, the purpose of a career civil service in a democratic system is to carry out the various functions of government defined by the legislature, courts, and elected administration as being in the public interest. Reliance on financial incentives to accomplish that can be seen by some as being too entrepreneurial and, therefore, in conflict with the concept of a professional corps of public administrators conscientiously executing the policies of an elected administration in a way that best serves the public, not personal financial gain.

Second, partisan and ideological sentiments about the proper role of government in American society—sentiments that often tend to devolve into positions that either promote or discourage professional public service as a career choice—influence attitudes in a particular elected administration about what level of reward is appropriate for exceptionally performing government administrators. Some believe such performance should be incentivized and rewarded above standard salary levels; others maintain that a high level of performance is just part of the administrator's job and not worthy of additional financial reward.

Finally, on the individual level, motivation to work in government can range from the altruistic desire to work for the public good to the personal predilection to seek relatively secure employment at the cost of potentially higher financial remuneration. As a generalization, people who make their careers in the public sector are not as motivated by money as those who choose the private sector. As a result, though monetary awards are always appreciated and no doubt have varying degrees of motivating value for different individuals, people in the public sector generally tend not to see them as a principal measure of success or an essential condition of continued employment.

There most certainly are monetary incentives available in the public sector, usually in the form of specified amounts tied to individual performance evaluation, group performance, and employee-suggestion systems that result in measurable financial benefits. These financial benefits, however, tend to be fixed and limited in amount because of the prevailing policy and political belief that any financial benefit derived from the efficiency of government operations should accrue largely to taxpayers in the form of reduced government expenditures. Thus, though the use of monetary incentives is not without value in government organizations on an individual or small-group level, it does not have the motivating push-tool power that one would typically expect it to have in the private sector because of the nonentrepreneurial nature of the public sector. So how do you build incentives into public sector organizations?

The limited power of monetary incentives coupled with the strong sense of job security that prevails across the government sector leave public-sector managers heavily reliant on pull tools. That is why the lessons of the previous chapters are essential. Getting off to a good start by understanding your mandate and the type of organizational situation you face, learning what is necessary, and forming constructive working relationships with your team and stakeholders is critical to establishing the sort of leadership strategy that will pull those who work for you and with you toward accomplishing your most important goals.

Designing an incentive system that depends heavily on pull tools is a challenge. The correct mix of individual and group incentives depends on the relative importance of independent and interdependent activity for your unit's overall success. What you must avoid is inadvertently setting up incentives that encourage the pursuit of personal goals when teamwork is necessary, or vice versa.

Establishing New Team Processes

Once the team and its goals, measures, and incentives are in place, the next step is to think through how you want the team to work. What processes will shape how the team gets its collective work done? Leaders vary strikingly in how they handle meetings, make decisions, resolve conflict, and divide up responsibilities and tasks.

The implication is that you should be careful not to plunge into introducing new ways of doing things too precipitously. If you are taking over an existing unit, for example, spend some time familiarizing yourself with how your team worked before your arrival and how well its processes worked. In doing this you can decide which processes you want to retain and which you want to change.

Assessing Existing Team Processes

How do you go about learning about your team's existing processes? As discussed earlier in chapter 3, talk with team members and support staff, and, where possible, meet or talk with your predecessor. Ask team members to brief you on their functions and to explain key processes. Probe for answers to these questions:

- **Participants' roles.** Who influenced your predecessor most? Who liked to play devil's advocate? Who avoided uncertainty? Whose opinions seemed to be most respected? Who was the peacemaker? The dissident?

- **Team meetings.** How often did your team meet? Who participated and who set the agendas?

- **Decision making.** Who made what kinds of decisions? Who was consulted on decisions? Who was informed once decisions were made?

- **Leadership style.** What leadership style did your predecessor prefer—how did he or she prefer to communicate, motivate, and make decisions? How does your predecessor's leadership style compare with yours? If there are marked differences between those styles, how will change likely affect the way the team is used to working?

Targeting Processes for Change

Once you are confident that you understand what has and has not worked well for your team in the past, it is time to apply that knowledge and establish the new processes you see as needed. For example, in our research we interviewed the head of a large federal agency who was brought in because the agency had had an embarrassing performance failure and was in need of a turnaround. One of the things the new agency head found shortly after his arrival was a twenty-page document spelling out in excruciating detail how decisions were made. Its effect was simply to diffuse accountability and paralyze the agency's ability to respond to problems.

The new executive responded by discarding that document and instituting a more direct system of group decision making. Many new leaders decide that their team's meeting and decision-making processes would benefit from revision, and, if that is the case for you, the sooner you begin spelling out the changes you envision, the better.

Altering Who Participates

One common team process problem—and a great opportunity to send a message that change is on the way—concerns who participates in key meetings. In some organizations, such as the agency we just mentioned, meetings tend to be too inclusive, with too many people involved in discussions. The result is inefficient decision making. In others meetings can be too restrictive, thereby sending a message of managerial unilateralism, excluding potentially valuable insights and perspectives on the matters at hand, and limiting broad accountability and buy-in for the decisions themselves. Balancing the need for efficiency with the motivational benefits of wide participation requires careful consideration of your unit's operating needs. A good approach is to structure meetings narrowly or widely, depending on the issues to be decided. As with most things in management, flexibility is key.

In Julie Davis's case, she wisely adopted an inclusive approach that invited equal participation by staff members at all levels. She was able to do so in part because her staff was small; when larger groups are involved, including representative "slices" of the organization might be the better approach.

Managing Decision Making

Many new leaders have difficulty establishing the best decision-making processes at the start. This happens because they have a style with which they are comfortable and they believe they must be consistent or risk confusing their team members. But there are several ways to make good decisions; the key to knowing which is best in a given situation and to communicating why to team members, is establishing a decision-making framework based on the nature of the decision itself. The possible approaches can be arrayed on a spectrum ranging from unilateral to unanimous consent, as illustrated in figure 5-2.

Sometimes decisions must be made either unilaterally or in consultation with just a few individuals. When that happens, of course, the risk is that you may miss critical information and insights and wind up with lukewarm support because others have the impression that only a favored few have influence. At the other extreme, processes that require unanimous consent tend to suffer from decision diffusion, going on and on and either never really reaching a conclusion or, if one is reached, settling for the least-common-denominator compromise. In either case, critical opportunities and threats are not effectively addressed. Between those extremes are the decision-making processes most leaders use:

- **Consult-and-decide.** When a leader solicits information and advice from a group or from a series of individuals but reserves the right to make the final call, he or she is using the consult-and-decide approach. In effect, the leader separates the process of information gathering and analyzing from the process of evaluating and reaching a conclusion, relying on the group for one but not the other.

- **Build consensus.** When the leader seeks information and analysis as well as buy-in for any decision, that is the build-consensus approach. The goal is not full consensus but sufficient consensus, meaning that a critical mass of the group believes the decision to be the right one and, importantly, that the rest agree that they can live with and support implementation of the decision.

FIGURE 5-2

The decision-making spectrum

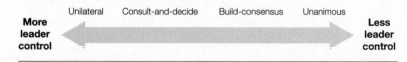

When should you choose one of these processes over the other? The answer is not, "If I am under time pressure, I will use consult-and-decide." Why? Because although it may be the quicker route to a *decision*, you will not necessarily reach the desired *outcome* any faster. In fact, you could end up spending more time trying to sell the decision after the fact or pressuring people to implement it. Those leaders who like to take quick action are most at risk of this; they want to reach conclusion by making a call but may end up jeopardizing their goals in the process.

The following rules of thumb can help when you must decide which decision-making process to use:

- If the decision is likely to be divisive—creating winners and losers—then you are usually better off using consult-and-decide and taking the heat. A build-consensus approach will just fail to reach a good outcome and make everyone mad at each other. Decisions about sharing losses or pain among a group of people are best made by the leader.

- If the decision requires energetic support from people whose performance you cannot adequately observe and control, then you are better off using the build-consensus approach. Consult-and-decide might be faster, but it also risks not getting the desired outcome.

- If you are managing a team of people who are relatively inexperienced, then you usually are better off relying on consult-and-decide until you assessed your team and developed their capabilities. Trying a build-consensus approach with an inexperienced team risks creating frustration, and you likely will make the decision anyway, thereby undercutting the effort to build teamwork.

- If you are put in a position of supervising people with whom you must establish your new authority (such as supervising former peers), then you are better off relying on consult-and-decide to make some early key decisions. You can relax and rely more on building consensus once your authority has been established.

Your approach to decision making also will be heavily influenced by which of the ST$_A$RS situations you are in. Start-ups and turnarounds are situations in which consult-and-decide works best as the problems tend to be technical rather than cultural or political in nature. Also, the staff might desire strong leadership to help them out; staffs often view consult-and-decide leaders as strong. In realignment or sustaining-success situations, on the other hand, leaders often have to deal with strong in-place teams and confront cultural and political issues. These sorts of challenges are usually best dealt with through the build-consensus approach.

To alter your decision-making approach to the nature of the decision being made, you sometimes will have to restrain your natural inclinations. You are likely to have a preference for either consult-and-decide or build-consensus decision making. But these are only preferences, not hard wiring. If you are a natural consult-and-decide person, you should experiment with building consensus in suitable situations. If you are a build-consensus person, you should feel free to adopt a consult-and-decide approach when you believe it is appropriate to do so.

To avoid confusion, consider explaining to your team members what approach you are going to use and why. Most important, whatever process you use must be seen as fair. Even those who may disagree with your decision often will support it if they feel that their views and opinions have been heard and sincerely considered, and if you have given them a plausible rationale for why you made the call you did. The flip side of this is not engaging in building consensus for a decision already made. This charade almost never fools anyone and just winds up damaging your precious credibility and the probability that your decision will be effectively implemented. You are better off just using consult-and-decide.

Finally, you can shift between build-consensus and consult-and-decide modes as you gain deeper understanding of people's interests and positions. It may make sense, for example, to begin in the build-consensus mode but reserve the right to shift to consult-and-decide if the process becomes too divisive. It also might make sense to begin with consult-and-decide and shift to build consensus if it emerges that energetic implementation is critical and consensus is possible.

Conclusion

Team building is arguably the most important, and is certainly among the most difficult, of the tasks facing new leaders. This is the case in both public- and private-sector organizations. But in government agencies the process is complicated by restrictive rules, imposed goals, and the unavailability of powerful financial incentives. Nevertheless, our research has revealed many cases of extraordinary leaders who, regardless of the constraints, have achieved success in motivating the people in their organizations to achieve new successes. The lesson that Julie Davis learned about the need for clarifying performance goals, for example, proved valuable both in terms of improving the performance of her organization and in demonstrating to her staff and key customers her skill as a leader in adapting to changing circumstances.

ACCELERATION CHECKLIST

1. What are your criteria for assessing team members' performance, and how do the members of your inherited staff measure up against them?

2. What personnel changes might be required and how soon?

3. What kind of help will you need with restructuring, and how will you preserve the dignity of the people who will be most affected?

4. How can you best employ existing incentive systems to motivate your team to its new goals?

5. What new team processes will you implement?

6. How will you make decisions—at first and later on?

6

Create Alliances

THE DAY Duane Robinson was sworn in as director of the state human services department, his boss, the newly elected governor, gave him a clear mandate. "Restore public faith," Duane was told. "And do it as fast as you can." This was a tall order. The department Duane was inheriting had come under fire during the previous governor's administration, after media exposure of a series of questionable financial-management practices and a heavily publicized failure in its handling of several child-welfare cases.

Duane had been a senior executive at a midsize private health-care company. He was known as an aggressive leader, someone who could move often recalcitrant bureaucracies to get things done. But he quickly began to wonder whether he had bitten off more than he could chew.

After just a few weeks, it was clear to Duane that he had inherited a very troubled organization. The recent problems, serious as they were, were just symptoms of much deeper dysfunction. There was a palpable lack of trust among senior managers and a culture of defensiveness that had virtually cut off essential communication between offices. During his first week Duane was sought out by several senior-level managers offering their views of the situation facing the department and advice on a range of internal personnel and operations matters. The views that he got were conflicting and, in some cases, downright hostile toward others in the organization.

Concerned, Duane embarked on a concerted effort to open up communication among his direct reports. He initiated weekly all-hands meetings, hoping to engage his staff in problem-solving dialogue. But discussions were strained at best, and people quickly retreated into defensive crouches. Duane sensed that most of the real discussion was happening outside the room, as warring alliances engaged in battles before and after his meetings.

After six weeks, Duane was fed up with the conflicting opinions and hostility among his direct reports. He wished he could replace the whole lot and start over, a course of action that was, of course, impossible given civil service restrictions and the pragmatic need to keep the place running. So he decided that the best approach was to administer shock therapy to the group.

He did this by falling back on his authority to simply force needed change. Over the next few weeks, Duane issued a flurry of directives defining new operating protocols and program-evaluation metrics, shifted around personnel, and conducted several woodshed sessions with employees at all levels where he laid out the new law. In those meetings, he more than once referred to himself as "the new sheriff in town."

After two months, the department was in chaos. Whereas before Duane's arrival its work was stymied by internal feuding and hypersensitivity to public exposure, now it descended into a state of paralysis. Employees, confused by all the new directives (which, of course, were not supported by their managers) and made wary by what they perceived to be their new director's punitive attitude, simply shut down.

At the same time, senior managers began complaining about Duane's leadership style to their allies in the legislature and beyond. Soon Duane's phone started ringing with calls from irate lawmakers and union representatives. The low point came when Duane received a call from the governor's chief of staff demanding to know what in the world Duane had done to take a bad situation and make it worse.

By this point, it had already become clear to Duane that he had erred badly in his approach and had dug himself into a deep hole. He had stopped digging, but could he put things back on track before the situation degenerated even further and cost him his job?

The Lone Ranger Trap

Too many new leaders in government fall into the same trap as Duane Robinson. They assume responsibility for organizations that are larger and higher-profile than the ones they previously experienced. Then they come under heavy pressure, some of it self-generated, to bring about quick and dramatic results. Frustrated by their ability to get things moving in the face of complexity and deeply entrenched problems, they fall back into what leadership expert Ron Heifetz described as a "lone ranger" style of authority-driven decision making.[1] Seduced by the belief that they can impel change to happen, they instead catalyze the formation of opposition, a phenomenon known as *reactive coalition building*.

The result is a deeply debilitating vicious cycle in which overreliance on authority yields increasing opposition that then encourages the leader to become even more authoritarian, and so on. Left unchecked, the result is a descent into an increasingly polarized conflict between the new leader and the existing staff and their allies. Given the new leader's vulnerability due to lack of knowledge and established alliances, and given that there usually are legal and political limits on making personnel changes, these are conflicts he or she is unlikely to win.

New leaders moving from the private sector to the public sector are especially at risk of falling into this trap. Why? Because leaders in businesses have clearer goals and metrics, more authority to hire and fire, and fewer external constituencies to deal with than their counterparts in government. They fail to understand the often complex relationships, for example, among agency-level managers, centralized executive authorities for budget, personnel, and administrative systems; and legislators who create the rules governing the way the system operates.

To avoid this trap, you must do more than just acquire the knowledge necessary to figure out *what* should be done. You must figure out *how* to do it; you must surmount the influence challenge. This means you must invest considerable time and effort early on to map the influence landscape and scope out critical coalitions.[2] You will need to identify individuals and groups, both inside and outside, who will exert influence on the future direction of your organization. In tandem with developing relationships with these people, you must find ways to build credibility and cultivate productive working relationships with key internal and external constituencies. With that base of constituencies, you must begin to create and communicate a vision for how your new organization should run. Key people must come to believe that you can lead the organization to a desirable future. Critically, you must create and sustain alliances in support of any major changes you hope to make. The balance between driving and restraining forces has to tip in your direction.

Mapping the Influence Landscape

Mapping the network of individuals and groups that exercise critical influence over government agencies is a complex process, but it is time well spent. Start by identifying influential parties and then dig deeper to diagnose networks of influence.

Identifying Influential Parties

The most obvious sources of influence are the vertical lines to your boss and to your subordinates. But don't fall into the trap of focusing all your attention up and down, and not enough side to side. One common mistake that new leaders make is to devote too much of their transition time to the vertical dimension of influence—upward to the boss and downward to subordinates—and not enough to the horizontal dimension, namely peers and external constituencies. This error is understandable; it is natural to gravitate toward the people to whom you report and who report to you. After all, they are the primary channels through whom you will have an impact and leverage yourself. However, as in Duane's case, focusing exclusively on your mandate—for Duane it was the direction given him by the governor—may lead you to seriously discount the interests of the other stakeholders involved and, as a result, place you in a vulnerable position.

Key horizontal relationships include individuals and groups inside your organization and beyond it. This means reaching out to peers, other employees, and such agency support functions as budget and finance. Although these people may be outside your immediate line of authority, they nevertheless exert significant influence over your operation. Consider as well the more remote executive agencies that control governmentwide budget and revenue matters and set personnel and procurement policies. Plan to reach out, as appropriate, to the legislatures and relevant oversight bodies, lawyers, public-employee unions, inspectors general and auditors, public affairs and freedom of information offices, and, of course, your ultimate public-service constituency. Table 6-1 and figure 6-1 lay out a typical list of points of influence and their individual chief interests, internal and external. A new leader should develop an awareness of how each one affects his or her new position.

It has been said that while the currency of business is currency, the currency of government is power. So for someone taking over a senior executive position in a public organization, identifying internal and external points of influence is not enough. A new leader also must understand the basis of power of each point of influence so as to gauge not only how but to what degree it will affect his or her performance. For some points, such as legislatures, executive agencies, and auditing or regulatory agencies, power is exerted through codified authorities over resources, administrative systems, and integrity issues that remain constant from elected administration to administration. For others, such as certain policy officials, constituent groups, and employee unions, power is derived from political affiliations that can ebb and flow over time. In any case, however, it is critical for the new leader to quickly grasp the sources of power for each major element on the influence map illustrated in figure 6-1 so that as he or she develops a leadership strategy and begins to target

TABLE 6-1

Internal and external points of influence and their chief interests

Points of influence/ chief interests	Internal	External
Bosses	• Performance goals • Teamwork and support • Compliance with laws, regulations, and policies	• Compliance with administration's policy • Integrity of reporting • No surprises/embarrassments
Employees	• Fairness in opportunity/ rewards • Clear direction • Approachability of boss	• Union contract negotiations and administration • Professional associations' safeguarding of standards
Peers	• Allies vs. competitors • Share vs. covet information • Trust vs. beware	• Advice-and-counsel network
Budget and finance	• Right allocation of resources • Performance measurements • Information gathering and reporting	• Implementation of administration's budget • Legislature's appropriation of resources
Human resources	• Effectiveness in recruiting, development, and compensation processes • Fairness and consistency of HR practices • Performance evaluation systems	• Compliance with governmentwide laws, regulations, and policies
Legal	• Legality of management actions • Advocacy in courts and administrative bodies • Ethics	• Adjudication of conflicts • Legislature's program oversight
External relations	• Management awareness of constituent group positions/ activities • Favorable media image • PR crisis management	• Advocacy of constituent interests • Media and other inquiries into agency operations and problems
Procurement	• Meeting organization's priorities for acquisitions • Compliance with laws, regulations, and policies	• Compliance with governmentwide procurement laws, regulations, and policies

FIGURE 6-1

Points of influence

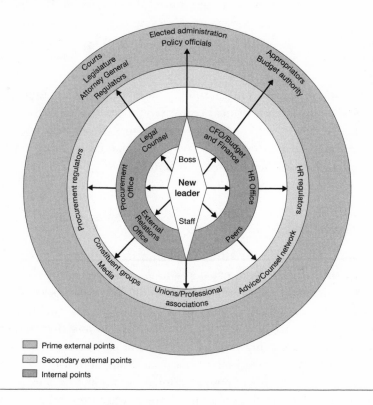

certain areas for improvement, he or she gives appropriate regard to what is controllable, what is negotiable, and what is a given.

How do you go about determining who will be important for your success? To a degree, it will become obvious as you get to know your new position better. But you can accelerate that process. Constituents, customers, and suppliers, within and without your agency, are natural focal points for relationship building.

Another strategy is to get your boss to connect you. Request a list of people outside your unit whom your boss feels you should get to know. Then set up early meetings with them. Remember, practice active listening while engaged in these discussions: ask evocative questions, and use what-ifs as a means to elicit thoughtful advice. If you are not satisfied with an initial answer, ask the question two or three different ways during the discussion, but avoid seeking self-fulfilling answers or triggering defensiveness with the way you ask your questions. If Duane Robinson had used this approach as he strove to gain information from his cadre of managers, he might well have stimulated discussion that was far less self-serving, far more enlightening, and much less frustrating for him. Had those early critical conversations gone better, it is less likely that Duane would have chosen to ignore the existing organization and fallen into the lone ranger trap that cost him so dearly in damaged credibility and lost momentum.

Diagnosing Influence Networks

Once you are armed with insight into some of the key players and their interests, your next step is to diagnose the influence networks which exist within every organization. These networks, often known as the "shadow organization," consist of discernable patterns of deference among people in institutions, and they matter greatly both in making change happen and in blocking change.[3] These influence networks exist because formal authority is by no means the only source of power in organizations and because people tend to defer to the opinions of others whom they either fear or respect or admire.[4] Reasons for deference include:

- Special expertise

- Access to important information

- Status

- Control of resources, such as budgets and rewards

- Personal loyalty

- Coalition partnering

The result is a set of informal channels for communication and influence that operate in parallel with the formal ones. Sometimes the informal organization supports what the formal structure is trying to do, and sometimes the informal organization subverts it.

To deepen your understanding of how influence works in your organization, you need to analyze these patterns of who defers to whom on a given issue, and the sources of power that underlie these patterns. You can use some of the accelerated learning techniques to gain insight into these political dynamics.

Eventually, you will be able to identify the *opinion leaders*—those who exert disproportionate influence through formal authority, special expertise, or sheer force of personality. If you can convince these vital individuals that your priorities and goals have merit, broader acceptance of your ideas is likely to follow. By the same token, resistance from these people could galvanize broader opposition.

You will also eventually recognize *power coalitions*—groups of people who explicitly or implicitly cooperate to pursue particular goals or protect particular privileges. If these power coalitions support your agenda, you will gain leverage. If they oppose you, you may have no choice but to seek to break them up or establish new ones.

Awareness of the shadow organization also will help you avoid the danger of being "captured" by the wrong people. Inevitably, the arrival of a new leader causes those who exerted influence under the old regime to jockey for favored positions in the new one. Among the many people vying for a new leader's attention will be those (1) who cannot help because they are not capable, (2) who are well meaning but out of touch, (3) who actually wish to mislead, or (4) who are simply seeking power. New leaders must exercise great care in deciding to whom to listen and to what degree. If you are not careful in remaining evenhanded and uncommitted early, you will inadvertently alienate good people and lose valuable opportunities to form alliances that not only support what you want to do but can actually help you accomplish it.

Was a shadow organization the cause of Duane Robinson's frustration? There is no doubt that his new agency was in political turmoil, and whatever factions already existed had hardened their positions and were ready for battle when Duane came on board. But what if Duane had taken the time to better grasp the intricacies of his organization's political advocates and opponents? If he had, rather than quickly resorting to the authoritarian leadership style that backfired so destructively, he would have been able to define more clearly the various factions and view each as a candidate for membership (and reward) in a supporting coalition. If he had identified the good guys, those supporting the kinds of changes he knew were needed, Duane would have established himself as a leader of a coalition, rather than someone acting alone. His chances for getting some early credibility-enhancing wins and for laying a foundation for longer-term success would have substantially improved.

Building Credibility

To paraphrase Tolstoy, all credible people are the same; all those who lack credibility have each become so in their own way.[5] In the world of government, credibility between professional managers and their bosses, their staffs, their peers, political executives, legislators, the public, and the media depends on several key elements, all of which must be present in some form in your leadership style.[6] The absence of any one or more of these principles will erode your credibility in its own way.

Recognizing the Key Elements of Credibility

When you first arrive in an organization, people will size you up and form early impressions based on relatively little data. To build credibility in your new position, you must first understand what *credibility* means to your new organization. What behaviors encourage people in the organization to perceive leaders as credible? What sorts of actions undermine credibility? Even if you are moving within your existing organization, you need to consider these questions. You may, for example, have been promoted to a new level with a different set of demands and expectations for leaders.

Listening and being known as a listener, for example, is a potent way to build credibility early on. Other key drivers include how you focus your time, how you treat people at lower levels in the organization, and what early decisions you make. In chapter 4 we presented a list of personal characteristics that enable new leaders to connect with their organizations and build the credibility they need to succeed. Because these characteristics are so important, we will revisit some of them here to reinforce how vital credibility is to leadership success.

In general, new leaders are viewed as more credible within their organizations when they are:

- **Honest in their statements and assessments.** Nothing will undermine your credibility with those whom you must lead faster and more permanently than insincerity in praise or criticism. Similarly, a new leader always must be forthright in his or her dealings with bosses, peers, and those internal and external stakeholders whose support is essential to success, even when those dealings involve conveying bad news.

- **Demanding but capable of being satisfied.** Effective new leaders press people to make realistic commitments and then hold those people's feet to the fire. A low tolerance for failure to meet commitments encourages people to make more realistic promises. But if you are never satisfied, you'll just sap people's motivation.

- **Accessible but not too familiar.** Being accessible doesn't mean making yourself available indiscriminately. It means being approachable in such a way that does not compromise your authority.

- **Decisive but judicious.** New leaders want to establish their ability to take charge, but appearing impulsive will get you in trouble. Early on, your goal should be to project decisiveness while deferring crucial decisions until you have learned enough about the issues involved.

- **Focused but flexible.** Avoid coming across as inflexible or unwilling to consider more than one way to solve a problem.

Effective new leaders establish their authority while encouraging input and consultation.

- **Active without causing commotion.** There is a fine line between getting things moving and overwhelming the organization. Leaders must be active without appearing unfocused or pushing people too far, too fast.

- **Willing to make tough calls but humane.** Most new leaders inherit at least one subordinate who needs to be moved, requiring an early tough call. Effective leaders don't shy away from doing what needs to be done; evasion sends a bad message. The key is to make delicate personnel moves in a way that is perceived as fair and that preserves the dignity of those involved.

Take a few minutes to think about your strengths and weaknesses in these principles. One important realization is this: while it is essential to be mindful of each of these principles, consistently striking the perfect balance between actions that build credibility and actions that erode it probably will not happen due to the immense variation in situations and people who you, as a new leader, will face. You are most likely to have a predilection for leaning to one side or the other in any given situation, so as you assess your credibility-building strategy, consider whether you are more at risk of:

- Being too frank or too tactful

- Being too accessible or too remote

- Being too demanding or not demanding enough

- Being too conservative or too impulsive

- Being too rigid or too flexible

- Being too energetic or not energetic enough

- Being unwilling to make hard personnel calls or prone to doing so in ways that could be perceived as inhumane

The drivers of credibility are determined partially by culture, which can vary significantly from organization to organization. But these questions can serve as a reference for thinking about building personal credibility with those whose support you will need most.

Duane's early actions resulted in a major early loss of credibility and the consequent need for him to reverse his course. His impatience with the shadow organization he inherited and his strong desire to quickly carry out his mandate from the governor pushed him into a no-win position where he was deliberately untactful, remote, demanding, overly energetic, and rigid. The destructive consequences of Duane's early actions could have been avoided if only he realized that building credibility as a leader was not a matter of demonstrating his authority. Rather, it was a matter of learning, planning, reaching out to key internal and external constituencies, and building alliances to support the changes he knew had to be made.

Setting the Tone

Given your analysis, what are the implications for the tone you need to establish in your new organization? Try to distill out a few important themes or messages that you want to convey. Research has demonstrated that communication is more effective if you can develop a few clear messages and then repeat them, in one-on-one meetings and group contexts, until they sink in. It's like composing a good piece of popular music. The key is to come up with a memorable melodic hook.

As you seek to communicate your messages, keep in mind that your early actions will also have a powerful impact on initial impressions. Early actions often get transformed into stories, which can define you as a hero or villain. Do you take the time to informally introduce yourself to the support staff, or do you focus only on your boss, peers, and direct reports? Something as simple as talking to people can help brand you as "accessible" or "remote." How you introduce yourself to the organization, how you treat support staff, how you deal with small irritants—all of these pieces of behavior can become the kernels of stories that circulate widely. "This was probably the most important message I sent at the beginning," noted one executive we interviewed. "The staff was used to an older, hands-off style of management where the former leader was not accessible or open to ideas. I wanted to send the message that we were going to have a culture of listening, gathering ideas, following up, and executing."

This is another opportunity to look for and leverage teachable moments. Remember: these need not be dramatic statements or confrontations. They can be as simple as asking the penetrating question that crystallizes your staff's understanding of some key problem. Duane Robinson missed this crucial opportunity by quickly adopting an authoritarian approach when he became frustrated with the dissent among the agency's staff. His message was an intimidating one, which led to myriad bad stories about him that quickly circulated throughout the agency and that ultimately suppressed both performance and communication.

Developing and Communicating Your Vision

Effectiveness in building credibility lays the foundation for the next step: developing and communicating your vision of what the organization could become.[7] To do this, it is important to understand what an effective vision is and how one is best developed.

Elements of an Impactful Vision

To have impact, a vision must encompass three key elements: consistency with the new leader's priorities, linkage to core values that provide meaning and purpose, and embodiment in crisp statements that evoke compelling mental pictures.

Consistency with Priorities. The vision must, of course, be consistent with the priorities the new leader has defined for the organization. These flow directly from the expectations of your new boss and the strategies you develop. Priorities make two essential contributions to the formation of a vision. First, they offer milestones that provide a way of tracking progress in achieving necessary new behaviors. Second, the discipline of defining priorities and aligning the vision with them makes the resulting vision more practical and tangible.

Linkage to Core Values. An effective vision is built on a foundation of values—such as integrity and loyalty—that imbue it with meaning and provide a sense of purpose.[8] Values such as loyalty, commitment and contribution, individual worth and dignity, and integrity are core values new leaders can draw upon in developing their visions. Other examples of core values include:

- Loyalty
  - Commitment to an ideal
  - Sacrifice to realize that ideal
- Commitment and contribution
  - Service to the public
  - Creating a better society or world
- Individual worth and dignity
  - Respect for the individual, including eliminating exploitative/patronizing practices, treating people with decency, and providing opportunity for all
  - Providing the means for each person to reach his or her potential
- Integrity
  - Ethical and honest behavior
  - Fairness in all interactions
  - Respect for the spirit as well as the letter of the law
- Achievement
  - Drive for excellence, quality, always doing one's best, and continually improving
  - Providing challenging opportunities for people

- Affiliation
  - Always thinking of the good of the team
  - Creating a climate where employees can do personally rewarding work, especially in groups
- Impact
  - Having impact and control
  - Giving recognition and status to individuals or organizations

Embodiment in Evocative Statements. A vision should be embodied in crisp statements that evoke compelling mental pictures. These statements should embody the priorities and core values and describe in graphic terms the way the organization should be: how it will be organized, how it will look different from how it looks today, what will be seen and heard, and what it will feel like to work in and with it. An example of a compelling vision statement might be, "I see people working intelligently and hard to get the job done and, by doing so, showing that they have a sense of duty to the mission and to serving the public."

Developing Your Vision

Creating a vision for the future in the complex operating environments of most public-sector organizations is quite different from doing so in the corporate world. As we have pointed out, in government the missions, authorities, and in some cases even resource levels of individual departments and agencies are spelled out in law, regulation, and executive order that are beyond most executives' control or influence. In addition, the performance of most public organizations is subject to a high degree of transparency, and the often shifting or impatient public scrutiny that results from such exposure can bring to bear indirect pressure for deviation from otherwise soundly conceived strategies. More directly, not only are the stakeholders who exert primary influence over organizational performance much vaster in number than those usually found in the business world, but they also present a more highly diverse and competitive set of interests, complicating the process of envisioning a single future. It has been said that the problem with the future is that there are so many of them. Irrespective of these difficult conditions, you will need a vision that your staff and your bosses share in and can use as a lodestar for calculating progress and resource requirements.

In developing such a vision, the major trap to avoid is isolation. The wise new leader must, of course, be clear on the nature and applicability of constraining conditions, such as those we just alluded to, and on the core elements of the vision that for various reasons are nonnegotiable. But beyond these inviolable elements, the vision statement must be flexible enough to consider others' ideas and allow them to have input and to influence the vision process so that they share ownership. Like Duane Robinson, it often is tempting for new leaders to eagerly implement changes and achieve performance improvements to proceed with their own vision. Needless to say, working the vision-development process through staff, bosses, peers, and other interested parties is time consuming, can be frustrating, and often requires compromise. Nevertheless, if the vision is to take hold as a guide to the future, it must carry the concurrence of the people who will do the work or provide the support necessary to achieving it. Duane let his initial frustration drive him away from a participative approach that would have vastly increased the odds of his securing some key early wins, and of beginning the process of constructive change within the agency. Duane didn't force change upon the organization by going it alone; instead, the organization forced change upon him.

Creating and Sustaining Alliances

As you develop a deeper understanding of your new organization, you will reach the point where you will begin to identify initiatives that you will pursue to secure early wins. But for each significant initiative you pursue, you will face an associated influence challenge: How will you build and sustain a coalition in support of your priorities?

Identifying Supporters, Opponents, and "Convincibles"

Building alliances entails identifying and activating existing or potential supporters. These may be people who share your vision for the future, staff who have been quietly working for change on a smaller scale, or other new leaders who have not yet become acculturated to the status quo.

Building such alliances also means being aware of who your opponents are and their reasons for opposition. They may believe that you are wrong. Or they may have other reasons for resistance to your agenda, such as:

- **Comfort with the status quo.** They resist changes that might undermine their positions or alter established relationships.

- **Fear of looking incompetent.** They fear seeming or feeling incompetent if they have trouble adapting to the changes you are proposing and perform inadequately afterward.

- **Threat to values.** They believe you are promoting a culture that spurns traditional definitions of value or rewards inappropriate behavior.

- **Threat to power.** They fear that the change you are proposing would deprive them of power.

- **Negative consequences for key allies.** They fear that your agenda will have negative consequences for others they care about or feel responsible for.[9]

When you meet resistance, you should try to grasp the reasons behind it before labeling people as implacable opponents. Understanding resisters' motives will equip you to counter the arguments your opponents marshal against your initiatives. You may find that you can convert some early opponents. For example, you may be able to address fears of incompetence by helping people develop new skills. You also may find ways to compensate potential losers to make change more palatable. There are practical limits on your ability to win over resisters; sometimes the price is simply too high. But it is always worth asking yourself whether you can offer trades or other forms of compensation, such as advocating for an initiative they care about, to win support.

Finally, you should identify the *convincibles*, those who may be indifferent to or undecided about your plans, but who might be persuaded to support those plans if you can figure out how their interests might be blended with yours. This is where your effort to build credibility can yield additional dividends.

Developing relationships with those whose resources or connections you need to succeed is not a matter of cordiality. In public organizations, alliances are formed for an organizational purpose, and framing compelling arguments that motivate supporters, ameliorate the opposition, and push the undecided to your side depend not only on the quality of your ideas but on whether you are trusted.

Convincing the Convincibles

To convince the convincibles, you need to understand their interests and then craft persuasive arguments. These can be based on logic and data, on values and the emotions that values elicit, or on some combination of the two. Reason-based arguments have to directly address the pragmatic interests of the people you want to convince. Value-based arguments aim to trigger emotional reflexes.

But what if your very best efforts to build trust and offer logical and value-laden arguments fall short of moving people whose support you need from where they are—comfortable with the status quo—to where you wish them to be? When this is the case, you need to use additional techniques to build momentum: entanglement and sequencing.

Entanglement. *Entanglement* means moving people in desired directions in small steps and leveraging small commitments into larger ones over time. For example, if you are trying to launch a new initiative, begin by getting people to agree to participate in an initial meeting, then to doing a small piece of analysis, and so on. Entanglement works because each step creates a new psychological reference point for deciding whether to take the next step. Getting people to make commitments in public or in writing, tends to lock them into a course of action that makes later backsliding all the more difficult for them.

A related technique for overcoming initial resistance is to employ a multistage approach to problem solving. Start by getting people to take part in shared data collection relating to some problematic aspect of organizational performance that you picked up on during your learning efforts. Then shift focus to gaining a shared understanding of what the problem is and what its possible causes are. Then move into working out a solution strategy of which all parties involved can claim proprietorship and thus become stakeholders in its success.

Finally, there is the approach of employing behavior changes to alter resistant attitudes. At first glance this may seem counterintuitive—after all, don't people behave the way they do because of attitudes they have? Actually, the attitude-behavior equation runs both ways. It is possible to alter people's attitudes by compelling arguments, but it also is possible to alter attitudes through changing behavior in desirable ways because people feel a strong need to preserve consistency between their behavior and their beliefs. For instance, only two or three decades ago, leadership positions in government held by women or minorities were viewed as rarities, and with some skepticism about how such a change from the well-ingrained practice of white male preference might work in actual practice. Now, after concerted efforts to remove barriers for women and minorities throughout government, it is the skeptics who are rare. The lesson is that it often makes sense to get people to act in new ways rather than try to change their attitudes. More often than not, if you get them taking the right actions, the right attitudes will follow.

Sequencing. As we have seen, people routinely look to others in their social networks for clues about "right thinking" and defer to others with expertise on particular sets of issues. To the extent you understand patterns of deference, you can leverage this knowledge into disproportionate influence on a group by employing what David Lax and Jim Sebenius termed a "sequencing strategy."[10] The order in which you approach potential allies and convincibles will have a decisive impact on your coalition-building efforts. Why? Once you gain one respected ally you will find it easier to recruit others, and as you recruit more allies your resource base will grow accordingly. With broader support, the likelihood increases that your agenda will succeed, making it easier still to recruit more supporters. A key ally might be an especially influential employee, a formal group leader, a union officer, or an informal group leader whom other group members look to for guidance.

If you approach the right people first, you can set in motion a virtuous cycle of coalition building, as illustrated in figure 6-2. Your decision about whom to approach first, therefore, is a very important one and should be carefully considered.

Considering the approaches outlined above, one can see an alternative path that Duane Robinson could have taken to improving his agency's public image and level of professional performance. Suppose that, rather than yielding to his frustration, he had

FIGURE 6-2

The coalition-building cycle

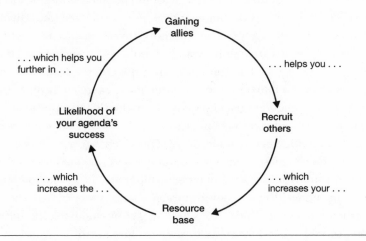

stepped back after his disappointing first round of conversations with his direct reports and reset his strategy. Still under pressure from the governor to quickly restore public faith in the agency, Duane nevertheless might have adopted a coalition-building approach and—instead of resorting to authoritarianism, punitive rhetoric, and threatening actions—he could have made some early judgments about who among his key staff members were convincibles. Building on a relationship with them, Duane could have employed an entanglement approach in enlisting support from the others, leading to a more participative process for the development of a vision and a strategy for getting the agency out of its morass. The governor might have been impatient with this approach, but convincing the governor of its merits was part of Duane's job, after all. And besides, which is worse: some moderate impatience with which Duane would have had to deal, or the danger of being relieved of his post—a distinct possibility resulting from the approach Duane actually took?

Conclusion

Whether you are assuming your first management position, moving to a higher level of middle management, or gaining responsibility for an entire agency, building credibility with the people whose support is necessary to carrying out your agenda is an essential first step. Duane Robinson elected to rely on sheer authority to create the changes that were necessary to carry out his mandate, but he soon understood that authority on its own has quite limited, if not counterproductive, effects. Just as it is imperative to invest time and energy to acquire the right sets of organizational knowledge from the right people, it also is vital to devise and employ strategies to build support and, conversely, stymie opposition before undertaking a major change agenda. Whose support do you most need? What influence networks are most important to you? Who are your potential supporters? How can you convince the undecided, and how can you sequence your actions to build momentum for your initiatives? These are key questions to examine as you proceed to build the support you need to succeed.

As for Duane Robinson, let us assume that, as an able executive and a quick learner, he took the lessons from his disastrous start and redirected his efforts toward building the kind of internal and external leverage he needed to restore his agency to its previous position of effectiveness. Duane's case, as with a few others we will discuss later on, is especially instructive because, as we have explained, had he pursued a different course, the whole debacle could have been avoided. It is our hope that by reading and using this book, you will not fall into these kinds of traps that set you back right from the start.

ACCELERATION CHECKLIST

1. Whose support do you most need to succeed?

2. What influence networks are most important to you? Who defers to whom on key issues?

3. How should you best approach building credibility? What does *credibility* mean in your new position? Does it differ among key constituencies?

4. What is a compelling vision for your new organization, and how can you best develop and communicate it?

5. Who are your potential supporters? Potential opponents? Convincibles? How will you test your hypotheses about support and opposition?

6. What tools of influence will you employ to convince the convincibles?

7. How will you keep in touch with key constituencies and ensure that a critical mass is comfortable with your efforts?

7

Achieve Alignment

WHEN THE AGENCY director returned from the first meeting he and his peers had with the department's new secretary and immediately called the senior staff together, Elaine Trevino, the assistant director for management, knew they were in for some big news. Secretary Reese Fuller, coming into government after a fast-rising career in the financial-services industry, made it clear during the run-up to his nomination that he did not intend to lead the department in a business-as-usual style, and during his confirmation hearings, his intention received strong support from the legislators on the agency's oversight committee. So, naturally, there was palpable tension in the room as the senior agency executives gathered to hear the director's report.

To everyone's surprise there was only one word on the director's agenda placed before each chair around the table: "Change." Somewhat puzzled, the executives leaned forward around the conference table and waited to hear what it meant. "Ladies and gentlemen," the director began, "after almost fifty years of carrying out its mission in essentially the same way, this agency is about to undergo a fundamental restructuring. Secretary Fuller calls it 'customer-based government,' and it is his stated goal to implement this new approach to providing better public services within a year. The good news is that it does not rely on outsourcing and that a pledge has been made to employee unions that there will be no layoffs because of this effort. The challenge, however, is that we, along with every other agency under Secretary Fuller's leadership, will now compete with businesses in the private sector for a large chunk of services we have been providing. It should be clear to everyone in this room that in order to come out on top in this competition we must shift our thinking and our ways of operating to become more entrepreneurial and more customer focused."

The director then turned and looked directly at Elaine. "As assistant director for management," he started, "I want you to do a fast but thorough analysis of what changes are needed in the way we are structured and the ways in which we now carry out our mission in order to position us for this new competition—competition with people who may be experienced in the methods and strategies of success in the marketplace, but who do not, as we do, have the depth of knowledge about the work we carry out. I look at this as an even playing field, and I believe that Secretary Fuller means it when he says he is not biased either way; his goal is better delivery of government services, regardless of who provides them. So, ladies and gentlemen, I believe that we have all the talent and other resources we need to succeed, and you may be certain that I have no intention of losing out in this competition. Each of you—as well as every employee—will have an important role to play in planning for and ultimately achieving our success. I am passing out the secretary's memo that details the strategy for customer-based government. Please note that he is willing to suspend some of the regulations that could interfere with our restructuring for competition so long as our implementation plan makes sense. Elaine, I'd like your report in a month."

As the senior staff huddled in the corridor outside the director's conference room and leafed through the secretary's memo, Elaine picked up on the usual mixture of reactions—cynicism, anxiety, and excitement. She had worked at the agency for almost ten years and was well familiar with its culture, its work systems, and the professional dedication of most of its employees. While she was confident in the agency's basic capability to take on this new challenge, she was not naive about the kinds of changes that would have to be made to convert this large, rule-based monopoly into a quick-footed, flexible organization able to compete with the best that the business world had to offer. She was excited by the prospect, and her mind was filled with ideas before she even reached her office.

The first thing she did was enumerate the major goals for the agency's implementation of the customer-based government (CBG) initiative: improve customer service; lower operating costs; increase flexibility in the use of resources to promote the pooling of skills, tools, and information; and streamline the entire organization to eliminate duplication and other structural drags on productivity. She then turned her attention to the problems.

As a typically organized government bureaucracy, the agency operated strictly by its organization chart and its carefully delegated authorities, all of which were designed to provide a stable, auditable mechanism for it to deliver services to its client agencies and justify its resource requirements to the executive and legislative bodies that controlled its budget. What such a structure could never do, however, was readily accommodate the kind of flexibility that was needed to succeed in an environment where the agency's clients had the option to procure their services from another source.

Elaine spent the next two weeks reaching out to her peers, employee groups, and constituents, discussing the goals of the CBG strategy and soliciting ideas for its implementation. She also met with several academics whose research on organizational change provided her with insights into the dynamics of the transformation process. Then she began to prepare the report the director was expecting. When she finished, she knew that her findings and recommendations would, if implemented, create a period of turmoil within the agency. But she was convinced that the problems she identified and the strategic changes she proposed would position the organization not only to survive but to prosper in the new competitive environment of customer-based government.

Her proposed strategy had four elements:

- Introduce risk into agency operations by allocating portions of the agency budget to its clients to use in procuring the

services the agency, as well as its potential competitors, provided. (This, Elaine believed, would stimulate creativity in
reengineering work processes, reducing costs, and improving overall productivity.)

- Merge several of the agency's existing support organizations
  into a single entity responsible for the new functions of bid
  preparation, performance measurements, and customer
  relations.

- Revise the existing compensation and incentive plan so it
  was more closely linked to performance.

- Convert the agency's funding method from an appropriation system to a self-sustaining working capital fund that
  would support cost accounting, facilitate billing, value productivity improvement measures, and provide a financial
  P&L-type reporting system that measured revenues as well as
  expenditures.

In her report to the director, Elaine acknowledged the myriad
technical difficulties in quickly implementing the strategy she recommended for redesigning and reorienting the agency so that it
was better aligned to meet its new challenges. She insisted, however,
that the main obstacle was not technical but cultural. The agency's
success in transforming itself would ultimately depend on behavioral changes at every level; implementing those changes, Elaine
emphasized, was the principal challenge the agency faced. One
week later the director gave Elaine the green light, and the real
work began.

The Leader as Architect

The role of architect is unlikely to be a familiar one to most new
leaders. Few managers get training in systematic approaches to
organizational design because they typically have limited control
over it in the beginning of their careers. It is commonplace for less
senior people to complain about poor organizational design and

to wonder why higher-ups let obviously dysfunctional arrangements continue. By the time you reach the middle-management levels of most organizations, however, you are well on your way to being complicit in the same tolerance of poor organizational structures that you earlier criticized. You are, therefore, well advised to begin learning something about how to assess and design efficient and effective organizations as soon in your career as possible.

Why? Because even the most perceptive, motivated, and charismatic of leaders cannot hope to accomplish much if the strategy is the wrong one; if the structure of the organization misdirects employees' attention or, worse, contributes to conflict; if key processes and systems are inefficient or unreliable; if the organization's skills are inadequate for the mandate at hand; or if the culture somehow inhibits the leader's ability to institute change. Your overarching design goal, therefore, is to align the architecture with your objectives and the demands of the external environment as defined in the organization's mission and objectives.

What is organizational architecture? It is the sum of these five critical elements, each of which represents an essential building block of any organization:[1]

- **Strategy.** The core approach that your organization will use to accomplish its goals.

- **Structure.** How people are situated in units and how their work is coordinated, monitored, and rewarded.

- **Systems.** The work processes used to carry out the organization's assigned responsibilities.

- **Skills.** The capabilities of the various groups of people in the organization.

- **Culture.** The values, norms, and assumptions that surround the other four design elements and shape behavior.

Misalignments among any of these five elements can render even the best strategy useless. Though strategy drives the other four, it also is heavily influenced by them. For example, if you need to realign a previously successful organization, as Elaine Trevino did, you likely will have to alter strategy and bring structure, systems, skills, and culture into alignment with the new approach. So clarifying your strategy and aligning the supporting elements must go hand in hand.

Viewing Organizations as Systems

If you hope to be effective as an organizational designer, you first have to understand what you are designing and how different design choices interact to affect performance. The point of departure involves understanding that organizations are *open systems.*

Open refers to the reality that organizations are profoundly influenced by their external environments. In the case of government organizations, mission and objectives are strongly shaped by the public environment, the demands of key constituencies, and the constraints imposed by laws and regulations. Closed systems are those where all the action happens inside and all the relevant variables can be controlled; they are obviously easier to design and manage. Every organization is an open system that strives to achieve closure by devising ways to control key elements of its external environment. Closure, however, never really happens with organizations; external influences always must play a vital role in organizational design.[2]

The *systems* part of *open systems* refers to the fact that, as illustrated in figure 7-1, organizations are made up of the five distinct design elements noted above, which interact. This has two major implications for your role as organizational architect. First, you can't change one element without carefully thinking through the implications for the others. The most common approach to changing organizations focuses first on changing strategy and then on bringing structure into alignment. This can be done reasonably quickly and is fine, so far as it goes. But significant changes in strategy and structure almost certainly will necessitate corresponding changes in systems, skills, and even culture. If these are not explicitly thought through and implemented, the organization will be out of balance, frustrating the efforts of many. Often these misalignments will get

FIGURE 7-1

Elements of organizational architecture

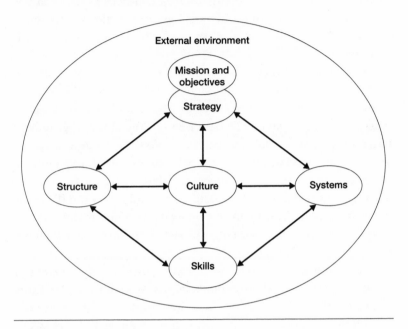

resolved, but only after much frustration and loss in productivity. So if you are planning to change strategy and structure, think of it as phase one, with phase two being a similarly disciplined effort to work through the implications for systems and skills. Culture, the final element of organization architecture, will shift slowly in response to your efforts to alter behaviors and to change the other elements of organizational architecture.

The second implication of the organizations-as-systems model is that it is possible to initiate significant change from any of the four "compass points" in figure 7-1. As mentioned, a common sequence involves changing the strategy first, the structure second, and then (hopefully) working through the implications for systems and skills. But it also is possible, and sometimes more effective, to initiate change by focusing on systems and skills. Process reengineering, for example, can be a powerful tool for streamlining organizations, so long as the implications for skills, culture, and structure are thought through. To the extent that organizational processes perform better, process reengineering can even have implications for strategy, because the organization is able to do things that it previously couldn't.

There are many ongoing examples of public-sector organizations working to align structure and strategy. For example, the Internal Revenue Service had endeavored for over a decade to upgrade its data-processing capability to better review the almost 250 million federal tax returns it receives each year. For many reasons, not the least of which was constituent and political opposition to a more effective IRS, the effort did not succeed in developing and implementing such new technology. But then, in the mid-1990s, the IRS came under increasing pressure from Congress and others to depart from its traditional law-enforcement approach and move toward a more customer-oriented strategy.

Under the leadership of a new commissioner with extensive business experience, the IRS made large investments in communication technologies designed in large part to put its agents and technical-assistance personnel into closer contact with taxpayers. Combined with modernized auditing technology, the culture of the IRS—often referred to as the least popular agency of government—made a dramatic shift from a sole focus on enforcement to a mix of enforcement and customer assistance. While it still is not exactly beloved by taxpayers, the IRS today is a substantially different organization than it was, due largely to wise and well-targeted technology investments aimed at facilitating a new culture within this unpopular but critical government agency.[3]

It likewise is possible to initiate major changes by bringing people with new skills into the organization. The World Bank, for example, was once staffed almost exclusively with economists who, not surprisingly, believed in the power of economic models to determine how development should take place. Beginning in the mid-1990s, the leaders of the bank began a concerted effort to recruit other types of social scientists, such as anthropologists and sociologists, with their own models of how best to make development happen. Although it took time, this major shift in skill bases influenced the bank's structure, the processes through which it dealt with developing countries, and ultimately its fundamental strategy.

Identifying Misalignments

Organizations can end up misaligned in many ways. The challenges faced by leaders of the Internal Revenue Service and the World Bank represented different kinds of organizational misalignment. One of your goals early in your transition should be to identify potential misalignments and then design a plan for correcting them. Common types of misalignments include the following:

- **Structure and strategy misalignment.** Elaine Trevino's agency featured separate and often duplicative functions, inflexible and rigid staffing structures, differences in workload and productivity measurements, and poor internal transfer of information—all of which made it impossible for the agency to meet the secretary's new mandate. The structure was working against the agency's own future success and had to undergo dramatic realignment.

- **Skills and strategy misalignment.** Suppose you are heading a procurement office that has been tasked with acquiring state-of-the-art IT systems, which are integral to your agency's strategy of improving constituent service. Your staff, however, has no experience in competitively acquiring such systems. In this case, your group's skills do not match the requirements of the agency's strategy, and new learning will be required to bring those skills into line. This kind of misalignment was a major hurdle the IRS had to overcome in redefining itself as being customer oriented.

- **Systems and strategy misalignment.** Imagine yourself as an information-technology manager in a large state human-services agency. Recently passed welfare-reform legislation requires your agency to gather, disseminate, and, for the first time, *interpret* a new and elaborate array of state workforce data. Formerly, the agency's information strategy was simply to collect and distribute data; now, however, agency leaders are required by the legislature to interpret the meaning of the statistical findings and to recommend policy initiatives to further the reform's goal of reducing welfare rolls and increasing the employment rate of former welfare recipients. The management information system now in use is ten years old and cannot accommodate this new requirement because it is designed for the collection of data only and does not contain the software needed for analysis. Your organization's systems cannot support your agency's new mandated strategy. The World Bank faced this challenge; even after acquiring the new skills it felt were needed, it found that the existing delivery systems were inadequate and prevented the organization from carrying out its strategy.

To assess potential misalignments, the place to begin is strategy. If your organization's strategy is a good match with its stated mission and goals, then it will most probably create the level of public value that is intended. If there is dissonance between strategy, mission, and goals, however, the strategy must change. But how? And what about structure? Does the structure support the strategy? If not, what structural change is necessary? If so, what about the organization's systems, skills, and culture?

Crafting Strategy

In the introduction to this book we discussed the risks of entering a transition without a plan—we likened it to flying blind into a storm. This caution is as important for an organization undergoing change as it is for the new manager leading the change process. There is a necessary logic to organizational design that if ignored in haste or in disregard of the difficulties inherent in organizational change can make even the most well-intentioned efforts go awry.

First and foremost, be sure that you understand your agency's larger goals and its strategy for achieving them, and that you and your boss agree on what part in it you and your group are expected to play. Then take a hard look at how your group is positioned with respect to that strategy. Crafting a well-thought-out and logical strategy for your group—one that defines not only what it will do but also what it will not do—will enable you to accomplish your objectives and contribute to the agency's strategic goals as well.

In government, the fundamental strategic questions concern the mission of the organization, the interests of all the various stakeholders in your group's performance, the statutory or regulatory constraints within which you must operate, the extant skills and capabilities of your group, and the availability of the resources you need. Use the following list to sketch out the basics of your group's strategy:

- **Mission.** Businesses exist to create profits for their owners; government organizations exist to create public value. Accordingly, businesses use the bottom line as a common measure of success. The extreme variety of activities within government, however, yields major differences in the ways that public value is defined and measured from agency to agency. Accordingly, the strategy of a government organization will vary substantially depending on whether its mission is to provide services, to collect and analyze information, or to ensure compliance with laws and regulations. Customer orientation may be a desirable goal for the IRS, for example, but—if criminals and terrorists can be considered a law-enforcement agency's customers—not for the FBI. So the starting point for evaluating and crafting strategy involves asking important questions: What is my organization's mission? How is it expected to create public value? What does it take to ensure that this value gets created as efficiently and effectively as possible? Table 7-1 provides some examples of the ways in which governmental organizations create public value and the associated strategic imperatives. Note that your organization may actually have some units that do service delivery, some that do analysis and reporting, and some that

TABLE 7-1

Missions and strategic imperatives

Type of public organization	Mission	Examples	Strategic imperatives
Service delivery	Provide specified services to the public as efficiently and effectively as possible.	Health care agencies, infrastructure-development programs, financial services, information distribution, social service agencies	Efficient delivery, security and integrity, error minimization
Analysis and reporting	Provide policy makers with specified information and analysis.	Treasuries, budget authorities, intelligence agencies	Accuracy, timeliness, risk management
Oversight and compliance	Ensure that individuals and institutions comply with specified laws or regulations.	IRS, regulatory agencies, law enforcement	Effectiveness, fairness, crisis avoidance

do oversight and compliance. If this is the case, you should focus on identifying the missions and working through the strategy implications for each unit.

- **Stakeholders.** Who are the most important stakeholders influencing the way your group performs? In the public sector, these interests can run from the usual verticals of boss and subordinates (including public-employee unions), to the internal horizontals of critical support functions, and finally to the external environment of legislatures, budget and revenue authorities, constituents, and such influential public observers as the news media. Which of these have the most direct effect on your group's performance? Which are most reliant on your success for their own success? Which must be consulted when developing your strategy?

- **Constraints.** In public-sector organizations, things like mission, goals, organizational structures, and agency performance metrics oftentimes are spelled out by law or regulation, and changing them, if they can be changed at all, often requires approval at many levels. In the case of Elaine Trevino's agency, the new strategy promulgated by the secretary included a promise of some relief from constraining regulations. What latitude do you have to institute quick changes to your organization's strategy, structure, systems, skills, and culture?

- **Capabilities.** What is your group good at, and what is it not so good at? On which strengths can you build a strategy for improvement? Which marginally performing capabilities must be improved? Which must be created or obtained from outside the group?

- **Resources.** In government, the acquisition of people, money, and space more often than not requires long lead time and must go through several layers of evaluation before a decision is made about them. Assuming that you are granted what you sought, actually acquiring them also takes a long time due to procurement and personnel system requirements. So, with the exception of when a new leader faces those relatively rare instances of a start-up or somewhat less rare instances of a turn-around, the immediate availability of resources is likely not to be something that should be counted on; making do with what you have will probably be the rule at the outset.

After reviewing the basic elements of your group's strategy, the next step is to understand its logic. Again, history is important. Begin by reviewing whatever existing documentation you can get your hands on that describes your group's mission and its past plans. Then break down the plans into their component parts—for example, goals and objectives, staffing patterns, budgets, workload measures, work processes, performance measures, and reporting systems. Do the various components of the plans complement each other? Is there a logical thread connecting them? For example, is there an obvious connection between workload measures, staffing patterns, and performance measures? If the group's situation or mission is changing, are there plans in place to prepare the staff for the changes with new training or technologies? If the plans are good ones, these connections will be spotted easily.

Next, you should assess the existing strategy's adequacy in terms of whether it promises to provide the resources the group will need over the next year or two. Does the existing strategy help support your agency's goals? Will it empower your group to accomplish what it needs to do to succeed? To assess adequacy, first ask some

SWOT Analysis

SWOT analysis is arguably the most useful and certainly the most misunderstood framework for conducting strategic analysis. SWOT—which stands for strengths, weaknesses, opportunities, and threats—was originally developed by a research team at the Stanford Research Institute (SRI) between 1960 and 1970.[a] The research was stimulated by a desire to figure out why corporate planning methodologies—pioneered by DuPont in the 1950s and broadly adopted in industry—had failed.

By the early 1960s most companies in the United States and United Kingdom had corporate planning managers who were responsible for analyzing the environment and the organization and for developing strategic plans. The most important finding of the SRI research was that CEOs should not delegate the strategic-planning function, but rather should become their organizations' chief strategists and work with other senior-line executives to formulate and drive strategy, perhaps with process support from a corporate strategy group.

SWOT was developed as a practical tool to help senior executives fulfill this role. The essence of the approach consisted of juxtaposing analysis of internal capabilities (strengths and weaknesses) with assessments of external developments (threats and opportunities) in order to identify strategic priorities and to develop plans to address those priorities.

Unfortunately, the developers decided to name their method SWOT, with the implication that the analysis should be carried out in that order—first strengths and weaknesses and then opportunities and threats. This has created no end of problems for those who seek to use the methodology to drive strategy discussions in teams. The problem is that a discussion of organizational strengths and weaknesses can very easily become abstract, undirected navel-gazing in the absence of something to anchor the discussion. The result is that groups often stall trying to define their organization's strengths and weaknesses, end up frustrated and exhausted, and so give short shrift to critical developments in the external environment.

The correct way to approach the analysis is to start with the environment and then analyze the organization. This is illustrated in the figure below. The first step is to assess the organization's external environment, looking for both emerging threats and potential opportunities. Naturally, this assessment must be conducted by people who are grounded in the reality of the organization and knowledgeable about its environment.

After identifying potential threats and opportunities, the next step is to evaluate them with reference to organizational capabilities. Does the organization have weaknesses that make it particularly vulnerable to specific threats? Does the organization have strengths that would permit it to pursue specific opportunities?

The final step is to translate these assessments into a set of strategic priorities—blunting critical threats and pursuing high-potential opportunities. These are then the inputs to a more extensive strategic-planning process.

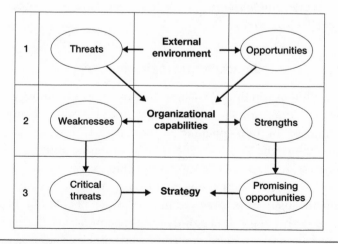

a. The research team included Marion Dosher, Dr. Otis Benepe, Albert Humphrey, Robert Stewart, and Birger Lie. See A. Chapman, "SWOT Analysis," Businessballs.com, 2005, http://www.businessballs.com/swotanalysisfreetemplate.htm.

probing questions of your boss and the staff about the sufficiency of resources available and the pragmatic probability of success under existing conditions. Then use the well-known SWOT method, to analyze the strengths, weaknesses, opportunities, and threats associated with the existing strategy. (See "SWOT Analysis.") Is your organization flexible enough to respond to changing conditions? Does it rely too heavily on dubious assumptions about acquiring new resources? Is there an organizational requirement not being met that your group could fill? Is your group in danger of marginalization due to outmoded technologies or inefficient work processes? The IRS arguably faced these types of challenges.

Finally, you should assess how well the strategy has been implemented. No matter how coherent the strategy is, or how intelligently it addresses future requirements, if it has not been implemented well, all is for naught. Are the performance measurements specified in the strategy actually used to make day-to-day decisions? Are the major goals of the strategy in line with what senior management really cares about? Are people cooperating across specialties as required? Is there sufficient training to provide people with the skills they need?

Answers to these questions will tell you whether to change the group's existing strategy or just the way it is being implemented. Chances are some modifications will be called for, so the next task is to decide how to do it.

Leading Strategic Change

Supposing that you discover major flaws in either the strategy or its implementation, can you radically change things without seriously disrupting your group's ongoing performance? The answer depends on two factors: the ST_ARS situation you are entering and your ability to persuade others and build support for your ideas.

Proposing significant changes to strategy is most difficult in realignment situations because you must convince people who believe they are performing well already that change is necessary. If, after evaluating the strategy in place, you conclude that the group is heading down the wrong path, your first job will be to persuade the boss and others that reexamining the strategy is necessary by asking such questions as: If we continue on this path, what might be the unintended consequences? Will the efforts needed to carry out this plan consume too many resources and crowd out more important goals? If, on the other hand, you conclude that the strategy will move your group in the right direction but neither fast enough nor far enough, the wisest course may be just to tweak it early on and plan for bigger changes later. For example, in the spirit of acquiring early wins to build your credibility, you might want to accelerate some training efforts or expedite the acquisition of a new technology. More fundamental changes should wait until you have completed your learning and built support among key stakeholders, many of whom will have to be convinced of the benefits and political feasibility of the changes you are proposing.

Altering the Structure

Once you have completed your assessment of your group's strategy and made whatever modifications you concluded were needed, you can address the question of whether the existing organizational structure supports the new strategy. What exactly is structure? Simply put, it is the way your group organizes people and processes—including technologies—to support its strategy. Structure consists of the following elements:

- **Units.** How the people you manage are grouped, such as by function, service, constituency, geographical region, or some combination of those.

- **Decision rights.** Who is empowered to make various kinds of decisions and how much discretion they have.

- **Reporting relationships.** How people observe and control the way work is done.

- **Performance-measurement and reward systems.** What performance-evaluation metrics and reward systems are in place and what incentives they create for people to do and not do.

- **Information-sharing and integration mechanisms.** How individuals and groups in the organization share information to make decisions and integrate their efforts to achieve the mission and strategy.

Before deciding to reshape your group's structure, carefully consider how these five elements interact. Does the way team members are grouped help achieve the goals? Who has the authority to make decisions? How is their work overseen? Are the kinds of achievements that matter most being measured and rewarded? Does information flow in the best way to facilitate efficient operations and decision making? Are there mechanisms in place to ensure that work in the "silos" gets integrated?

Unless you are in a start-up situation, where there is not an existing structure to assess, answering these basic questions about the way your organization is structured will position you to make correct decisions about changes that may be needed.

As you do this, keep in mind that there is no such thing as a perfect organization; every effort to design an organization necessitates making *trade-offs*. For example, leaders must always assess the trade-off between efforts to create internal efficiencies through cost reduction, staff cuts, and organizational consolidations that, while they may improve work processes, may end up impairing the organization's effectiveness in delivering the public services for which it was established. Ideally, an organization would be able to achieve all its various goals for efficiency and effectiveness, but in reality this is simply not possible. Public organizations often come under pressure to be "all things to all people." This inevitably undermines efforts and erodes capabilities. The organization that tries to be good at everything ends up being excellent at nothing.

Thus your challenge is to find the right balance for your situation. Here are some common problems you might encounter as you consider structural changes:

- **Is the team's knowledge base too narrow, too broad, or too dated?** When people of similar experience and training are

grouped together, they can accumulate deep wells of expertise, but they also can become compartmentalized and isolated from the mainstream of core work processes. Similarly,
groups with broad mixtures of skills may be more apt to be
integrated with core processes, but they may do so at the cost
of developing deeper experience. And if staff-development
plans do not stress keeping current in the technologies and
trends of the work, stagnation, with accompanying resistance
to change, will take hold.

- **Is employees' decision-making scope too narrow or too
broad?** Although centralized decision making is usually the
fastest method, it also usually excludes the advice and wisdom of others closer to the front lines who may be better
equipped to make certain of those decisions. On the other
hand, decision making spread out over a broad plane runs
the risk of being placed in the hands of people who will
make unwise calls because they do not understand the wider
consequences of their choices. A good general rule is that
decisions should be made by the people with the most relevant knowledge, so long as their incentives encourage them
to do what is best for the organization.

- **Are employees inappropriately rewarded?** This is a major
problem in public-sector organizations. Aside from the many
pilot programs instituted over the years to experiment with
pay-for-performance compensation plans, civil service rules
tend to reward individual tenure more than performance
and often work to encourage the pursuit of individual interests over group interests. Group awards are one possible
solution to this problem because such awards tend to focus
energy on team performance.

- **Do reporting relationships filter information flow?** Reporting relationships help observe and control the workings of
your group, clarify responsibility, and encourage accountability. Strict hierarchical reporting relationships might make

these tasks easier, but they can lead to a restrictive *stovepipe,* or vertical pattern, of information flow. More complex reporting arrangements like matrix structures can promote horizontal information sharing, but they can dangerously diffuse individual accountability and make performance measurement and reward difficult.

At Elaine Trevino's agency, the strategy adopted to reposition the organization so that it could effectively compete against private-sector providers touched on all these issues. The combined goals of becoming customer focused, concentrating on cost control, loosening the boundaries between units so that resources could be pooled, redesigning compensation plans so that they encourage higher performance, and eliminating structural duplication moved the agency away from its historically stable structure toward the more adaptive model envisioned by the customer-based government initiative.

Aligning Key Systems

Systems, also referred to as "processes," enable your group to transform information, materials, and knowledge into products or services that are essential for your larger organization as well as for other stakeholders. As with structures, you must begin by asking whether the processes currently in place support the strategy by enabling your group to meet or exceed the goals that it sets out.

The kind of processes required to carry out your strategy will vary with your goals. For example, if your major goals involve delivering existing high-quality products or services efficiently and reliably, there must be an intensive focus on developing processes that specify both the ends (productivity goals) and the means (methods, technologies, tools) in exquisite detail. But these same sorts of processes often have the effect of stymieing innovation. Therefore, if stimulating creativity is your major goal, you will need processes that focus more on defining ends and rigorously checking progress toward achieving them at key milestones, and less on controlling means. Performing a process analysis to map each system being employed within your group, identifying those that are most important to your strategy (your core processes), testing whether the related measurement and reward systems in place are appropriate, and identifying key bottlenecks is the first step toward achieving alignment between strategy and systems.

To evaluate the efficiency and effectiveness of each core process, you must examine four aspects:

- **Productivity.** Does the process efficiently transform knowledge, material, and labor into value?

- **Timeliness.** Does the process deliver the desired value in a timely manner?

- **Reliability.** Is the process sufficiently reliable, or does it frequently break down?

- **Quality.** Does the process deliver value in a way that consistently meets required quality standards?

When systems and structure jibe, the elements reinforce each other as well as the strategy. For example, a local government human-services agency structured so that trained teams work with specifically defined sectors of the constituent population (e.g., children, teens, young adults, parents, etc.) can incorporate a process by which information gathered by one team can be pooled and shared with all other teams. Such a formal information-sharing process can alert teams to others who might be facing similar or related situations, thereby elevating the performance of the agency as a whole. When systems and structure are at odds, such as when different teams compete for the same population using different approaches, they hamstring one another and subvert the larger group's strategy.

How do you actually improve a core process? Begin with developing a process map as mentioned earlier—a straightforward diagram of exactly how the tasks in a particular process flow through the individuals and groups who handle them. An example of a process map for a supply unit servicing an organization's material requirements is shown in figure 7-2.

FIGURE 7-2

Process mapping

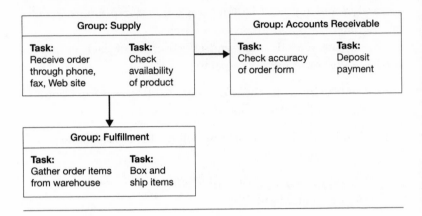

The team should study the map to identify bottlenecks and problematic interfaces between the individuals responsible for each set of tasks. For example, errors or delays may occur when the supply unit communicates the need for urgency in filling a material order from a production unit but the message gets lost on its way to the fulfillment group—process failures are common during hand-offs of this kind. Once a problem has been identified as interfering with the reliability of the overall supply process, the team should develop ways to reduce its recurrence.

Process analysis stimulates collective learning. It helps the entire group understand exactly who does what, within and between units and groups, to carry out a particular process. As indicated in the process failure example discussed above, process mapping also sheds light on how problems arise.

A few words of caution. You most likely are managing a number of processes. If so, manage them as a portfolio. Do not try to introduce radical changes in more than a couple of core processes at a time. Your group is not likely to be able to absorb much change all at once. As mentioned earlier, for instance, do not immediately automate problematic processes, a tactic that rarely solves the real problem underlying process inefficiencies. Problems with processes usually center on miscommunication, confusion over expectations, and misunderstanding about how the agency works. Solving deeper problems will yield bigger benefits than simply resorting to automation.

Developing Group Skills

Does your staff have the skills and knowledge they need to perform your group's core processes with excellence, and thus to support the strategy you have set? If not, the entire fragile architecture of your group could fall apart. A skills base is comprised of these four types of knowledge:

1. **Individual expertise.** Gained through training, education, and experience.

2. **Rational knowledge.** An understanding of how to work together to integrate individual knowledge to achieve specified goals.

3. **Embedded knowledge.** The core technologies on which your group's performance depends, such as information systems and databases.

4. **Meta-knowledge.** The awareness of where to go to get critical information—for example, through internal support functions or external sources of relevant knowledge or expertise.

The overarching goal of assessing your group's capabilities is to identify (1) critical gaps between needed and existing skills and knowledge and (2) underutilized resources, such as partially exploited technologies and unused expertise. Closing gaps and making better use of underutilized resources can by themselves produce substantial gains in performance and productivity.

To identify skills and knowledge gaps, first revisit your strategy and the core processes you identified. Ask yourself what mix of the four types of knowledge is needed to support your group's core processes. Then assess your group's existing skills, knowledge, and technologies. What gaps do you see? Which of them can be repaired quickly, and which will require more time?

To identify underutilized resources, search for individuals or groups in your unit who have performed much better than average. What has enabled them to do so? Do they enjoy resources—such as technologies, methods, materials, and support from key people— that could be exported to the rest of your unit? Have promising process-improvement ideas been tabled because of lack of interest or lack of resources?

Understanding the Culture

An organization's culture will shape how it approaches new problems—problems not dealt with within the existing bureaucratic structure. Since bureaucratic institutions and their rules are static and only serve to shape the present, they tend to have little to offer about how a bureaucracy should face new challenges and problems. Accordingly, leaders who must address such changing conditions are likely to be most influenced by the organization's cultural norms. In this regard, culture begins where rules end.

The central issue when seeking to understand the extant culture of a bureaucracy is drawing a distinction between its design, including rules and regulations, and its culture. As already noted, bureaucratic organizations are governed by written rules, and they are, to a large degree, defined by those rules because they serve to regulate behavior, distribute decision-making power, and establish the hierarchy of command that holds the bureaucratic organization together.

Organizational culture also is governed by rules, but not quite in the same way. Instead, it is governed by a set of unwritten *norms* that, though conditioned to some extent by organizational design, tend to be rooted in the ethos of the wider society to which the bureaucracy provides services. Norms, therefore, often are less easily discernable than the formal rules governing bureaucratic operations. This does not suggest that cultural norms are any less powerful than written rules when it comes to influencing the behavior of officials and others in the organization. To the contrary, culture often trumps rules, and that is why a new leader must understand it.

The culture that exists within a bureaucracy is shaped by internal and external forces. The internal forces are largely institutional, such as the organization's structural design and the norms by which it operates. For example, a culture of collaboration is often missing in a tightly stovepiped organization. To understand the external forces, however, remember our discussion earlier in this chapter about viewing organizations as open systems and, accordingly, carefully consider the wider culture of the world beyond the organization's boundaries.

Perhaps the most critical role played by any leader, and especially by those at an organization's highest levels, is one of interpretation; the rules may provide a framework within which to act, but they do not by themselves dictate decisions. Leaders, as well as all those others on their influence maps, are social beings and act beyond the specifications of rules. They have prejudices, interests, and fears in the same way that any individual has, and these factors, together with the prevailing cultural norms of the wider society, will influence how people work within the rule-governed framework. Therefore, leaders who are faced with alignment challenges must consider formal organizational structure and cultural norms equally.

Avoiding Common Traps

As you take on the role of organizational architect, keep in mind that too many managers rely on simplistic fixes to address complicated organizational problems. Be alert to these all-too-common pitfalls:

- **Trying to reorganize your way out of deeper problems.** Overhauling your group's structure in times of trouble can amount to straightening the deck chairs on the *Titanic.* Resist doing so until you understand whether restructuring will address the root causes of the problems. Otherwise, you may create new misalignments and have to backtrack, disrupting your group, lowering productivity, and damaging your credibility in the process.

- **Creating structures that are too complex.** This is a related
  trap. Although it may look good on paper to create a structure, such as a matrix, in which people in different units
  share accountability and in which creative tensions get
  worked out through those people's interactions, too often
  the result is bureaucratic paralysis. Strive whenever possible
  for clear lines of accountability. Simplify the structure as
  much as possible without compromising core goals.

- **Automating problematic processes.** Automating your
  groups' core processes may produce significant gains in productivity, quality, and reliability, but it is a mistake to simply
  speed up an existing process through technology if the
  process itself has serious underlying problems. Automation
  will not solve such problems and may even amplify them,
  making them even more difficult to remedy. Analyze and
  streamline processes first; then decide whether automation
  still makes sense.

- **Making changes for change's sake.** Resist the temptation to
  tear down fences before you know why they were put up. It is
  important for new leaders to respect the past. Those who
  feel self-imposed pressure to put their stamp on the organization often make changes in strategy or structure before
  they really understand the situation they face.

- **Overestimating your group's capacity to absorb strategic
  shifts.** It is easy to envision an ambitious new strategy. In
  practice, however, it is difficult for a group to change in response to large-scale strategic shifts. Advance incrementally
  if time allows. Focus on a vital few priorities. Make modest
  changes to your group's strategy; experiment; and then progressively refine structure, systems, skills, and culture.

- **Underestimating the importance of peripheral stakeholders.**
  In government agencies, the number of stakeholders, their
  range of interests, and the variety of their perspectives are
  usually quite extensive. So avoid falling prey to believing that

major structural changes can be made without doing important legwork—like coalition building or, at least, getting agreement among those stakeholders.

Conclusion

To be effective as a senior leader in government, you must be prepared to take on the role of organizational architect. This means cultivating your ability to observe and identify misalignments among strategy, structure, systems, skills, and culture. Draw on all this analysis to develop a plan for aligning your organization. If you are repeatedly frustrated in your efforts to get people to adopt more productive behaviors, step back and ask whether organizational misalignments might be creating problems.

ACCELERATION CHECKLIST

1. What factors concerning mission, stakeholders, constraints, capabilities, and resources need to be taken into consideration in crafting strategy?

2. How logical and adequate is the organization's existing strategy, and what changes do you think are needed?

3. What are the strengths and weaknesses of the organization's existing structure, and what changes are you considering?

4. What are the core processes of your organization, how well are they performing, and what are your priorities for improving them?

5. What skills gaps and underutilized resources have you identified, and what are your priorities for remedying them?

6. What are the functional and dysfunctional elements of the culture, and how might you begin to strengthen those that are a drag on performance?

Avoid Predictable Surprises

I T HAD BEEN two years since Carrie Brice's agency had been selected to receive the National Academy of Public Administration's Award for Excellence, one of just ten government organizations to be so honored. Since then she had participated in panel discussions and appeared as a conference speaker on the subject of "making government work" on several occasions. Inside the agency, an agricultural support services organization, the award was heavily promoted by senior management as evidence of the workforce's talent and dedication in carrying out reforms begun several years earlier. As the deputy director for field operations, Carrie had received special recognition for her role in the process. She had led a comprehensive field office restructuring that seemed on track to vastly improve service delivery. She was considered the prime candidate to replace the agency head, who was planning retirement within the year.

It therefore came as a shock when the director called her at home late one evening to inform her that six employees at the agency's Phoenix supply center had been arrested by local police and the FBI and charged with dealing in narcotics and stolen government property. After a sleepless night, Carrie arrived at her office at six o'clock in the morning and immediately began going through the audit and management review reports covering the Phoenix center's operations, as well as the regular monthly reports she received from the center's manager. Nothing in these reports gave even the slightest hint of irregularities in center operations.

As Carrie's shock morphed into anger, she was determined to get to the bottom of this costly and acutely embarrassing event. It had dangerous ramifications not only for the agency's reputation but also for her personal career aspirations. The arrests generated interest from the media, which attracted the attention of several members of Congress who served on the agency's appropriation committee. The department-level inspector general had no choice but to launch his own independent investigation of the Phoenix center.

Knowing that the agency would be dealing with the fallout from this for quite some time, Carrie was determined to get out in front of the crisis. She appointed a small investigative task force composed of her immediate and most trusted assistant, the agency's chief counsel, the head of human resources, and the head of security. She commissioned it with answering this basic question: why had there been no early warning of the situation?

As the external and internal investigations ensued, disturbing answers began to emerge. It became apparent that the agency's pride in its success, and its promotion of its reputation for excellence among its employees, had created a climate of self-congratulation. On the one hand, this helped reward the workforce for a difficult job well done. But on the other hand, it had sent a subtle and inadvertent message that any information that might contradict this positive image would not be welcome. First-line supervisors and middle managers, who were in the best sentry positions to spot irregularities, operated under the unspoken assumption that to deliver bad news was to incur disapproval from on high. So when confronted with suspicious circumstances, they tended to look the other way in the hope that what they suspected would never materialize into a real problem.

With only good news moving up the reporting chain, everyone, especially the supervisors and middle managers involved, was kept happy. The cost of this stifling filtration of critical information became painfully clear to Carrie and the other agency leaders as they digested the various investigative reports they received. In the senior managers' well-intended efforts to motivate and reward the workforce, as well as promote the agency's reputation for excellence among its peers and external stakeholders, they neglected a cardinal rule of preventing a predictable surprise such as the one at the Phoenix supply center: bad news is usually much more valuable than good news and is stifled at great risk.

Defining Predictable Surprises

A *predictable surprise* is an event or series of events that takes an individual or organization by surprise, despite prior awareness or availability of all the information necessary to anticipate the events and their possible consequences.[1] If you do not seek to identify, evaluate, and mitigate such ticking time bombs, all your efforts to plan for a successful transition and to lay the foundation for longer-term success could be for naught—because when those bombs do explode, all your energy will go into firefighting. Your hopes for systematically getting established and building momentum will be dashed.

Of course, true surprises really do happen. And when they do you simply must confront the consequences and surmount the resulting crisis as best you can. But far more often, new leaders are taken off track by surprises that really shouldn't have been surprising—if the warning signs were known and heeded. This often happens because the new leader, like Carrie Brice and her associates, simply doesn't look in the right places or ask the right questions.

We all have preferences about the types of problems we like to work on and those we prefer to avoid or don't feel competent to address. But as a new leader, you will have to discipline yourself either to dig into areas in which you are not comfortable or interested, or to find trustworthy people with the necessary expertise to do so.

In the complex operating environment of most government organizations, surprises can come from such *external* sources as political shifts, trends in public opinion, catastrophic national events, and quickly changing economic conditions—and from such *internal* sources as information system crashes, key personnel losses, individual

improprieties of various kinds, major product or service quality failures, and organizational political intrigue. In either case, it is essential
to regularly gather as much information as possible about those areas
that pose the greatest threats. Otherwise, you may find yourself facing
the very unpleasant task of dealing with a predictable surprise.

Sources of Vulnerability

What renders organizations vulnerable to being predictably surprised? Organizations become vulnerable when they lack the capacity
either to (1) sense and respond to emerging threats in a timely manner or (2) learn from experience and disseminate the resulting lessons learned to the right people and places. In the former case,
organizations—like Carrie's—fail to see emerging threats or are unable to mount an effective response in time. In the latter case, organizations squander opportunities to learn from experience—good and
bad—and so are doomed to repeat the same mistakes. We term these,
respectively, *sense-and-respond failures* and *learn-and-disseminate failures*.

How do organizations avoid falling prey to these failures? They
put in place processes explicitly designed to increase the organization's capacity to sense and respond and to learn and disseminate.
This is illustrated in figure 8-1. At the top of the figure is the sense-
and-respond (SR) loop, which consists of processes to recognize
emerging threats, establish priorities, and mobilize an effective
response. At the bottom of the figure is the learn-and-disseminate
(LD) loop, which consists of processes to learn from experience, to
embed the resulting insights into relevant parts (people and processes) of the organization, and to prevent people from forgetting.
The SR loop and the LD loop both draw upon and augment organizational capabilities.

To avoid predictable surprises, the SR loop and the LD loop
must operate efficiently (fast enough) and effectively (focusing attention and resources in the right ways). Each loop is necessary;
neither one on its own is sufficient to protect the organization. An
organization with an effective SR loop, for example, responds well
to emerging threats with which it has some previous experience.

FIGURE 8-1

SR and LD loops

Loop 1: sense and respond (SR)

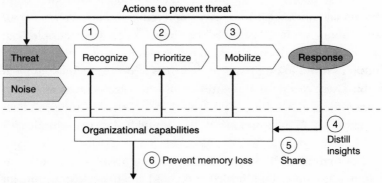

Loop 2: learn and disseminate (LD)

But if it lacks an LD loop, it cannot learn from sense-and-respond failures and do better the next time. Likewise, the capacity to learn from failures isn't worth much without the capacity to sense and respond to emerging threats.

Sense-and-Respond Failures

As illustrated in figure 8-1, the SR loop consists of three key sub-processes—recognition, prioritization, and mobilization. A failure in any of these can leave the organization vulnerable to being predictably surprised.

Recognition Failures

Some disasters can't be foreseen. No one, for instance, could have predicted in the 1960s that the HIV virus would jump the species barrier from monkeys to infect humans on such a vast scale. But many unforeseen disasters that strike organizations could and should be recognized because they happen for predictable reasons. These reasons include:

Preconceived Notions. Cognitive biases—systemic weaknesses in the way people observe events and make decisions—may blind individuals and organizations to emerging threats. Preconceived ideas about what is "possible" or "impossible," for example, can cause a leader to focus attention on certain types of problems while inadvertently allowing more serious ones to develop almost in plain sight. These recognition failures occur when leaders discount or ignore evidence that does not fit with their beliefs. Any time you hear someone say, "That's impossible," a warning bell should sound.

Confirmation Bias. A related problem arises when multiple, competing sources of information and analysis exist within an organization—one as large as the U.S. government or as small as a local public-service agency. When this is the case, some leaders will gravitate to assessments that confirm what they want to hear and tune out dissonant views. For example, media, congressional, and special commission scrutiny of intelligence gathering and analysis before 9/11 and the Iraq invasion fell into this trap and demonstrated how pervasive and crippling self-censorship was among those charged with identifying potential threats to national security.

This phenomenon is evident at all layers of organizations, and to win bureaucratic wars and retain influence with key decision makers, some leaders, like those in the first-line and middle-management ranks of Carrie's agency, quickly learn to tell those in power only what they want to hear. This failure can be reinforced by the complacency that comes when, despite mounting evidence, leaders believe that because the problem hasn't happened before, it probably won't happen now.

Inoculation. When the signals associated with a threat are masked by a high level of background noise, the result can be false alarms that "inoculate" leaders, making them resistant to seeing truly serious problems. By *signals* we mean clues, indications, and other evidence of serious vulnerability to an impending problem. *Noise* refers to conflicting information that points to other problems or presents more benign explanations for the threat. When the signal-to-noise ratio is low (i.e., when there are relatively few signals and a lot of noise), it becomes very difficult for even the most aware leader to distinguish genuine threats from false indications.

The signal-to-noise problem is further compounded by the organization's response to previous false alarms. Analysts tend to err on the side of caution—better to be chastised for being too cautious than for being too optimistic. This tendency among analysts may cause multiple false alarms and create "crisis fatigue" among leaders who grow leery of repeated warnings of problems that never seem to materialize. But when those responsible for scanning the environment allow themselves to drift from being overreactive to being underreactive, the organization as a whole may drift into perilous waters and become vulnerable to a true threat when one inevitably emerges.

Silos. Recognition failures also can occur because of the way organizations are structured. Most organizations have distinct silos that contain and vertically move valuable information. But often there are barriers that prevent information from being seen by other parts of the organization. Leaders must constantly make trade-offs between the need to create and protect these deep pools of expertise and information, and the need to integrate and synthesize information across the organization.

The simplest type of integration problem occurs when various members of an organization have pieces to the puzzle, but no one has them all—and, critically, no one knows who knows what. In short, the organization's knowledge never equals the sum of its members' knowledge. While various parts of the organization may have all the information necessary to perceive and deter a predictable surprise, no one person in the organization is capable of putting it all together.

In theory, senior management should play the role of synthesizer, compiling the information into the big picture to avoid stovepipe syndrome. But the barriers to this goal are great. There is immense pressure within bureaucracies to filter information as it rises through the hierarchy. The temptation to withhold or gloss over sensitive, confusing, or embarrassing information is great. Those at the top inevitably receive incomplete and distorted data, and overload may prevent them from keeping up-to-date with incoming information.

Illusory Consensus. Finally, organizations can suffer from illusory consensus, a problem rooted in the twin desires of most bureaucracies to avoid expending energy and incurring blame. It is all too easy, especially for the new leader, to interpret a lack of opposition to an initiative as positive support. Those who harbor doubts may keep quiet because they assume decision makers are armed with better information, or because they want to avoid accountability for mistakes. As soon as a predictable surprise occurs, however, those who were silent suddenly have an incentive to distance themselves from failure by going public with an "I told you so" message.

Illusory consensus is closely compatible with the concept of groupthink, which describes how members of an organization suppress their critical doubts and allow the false appearance of consensus to emerge. This is how Carrie and her associates got into the danger zone of ignorance without realizing it.

The mirror image of the illusion of consensus is suppressed dissent. Suppressed dissent can arise when one part of the organization is vested with *too much* responsibility for a particular issue and seeks to retain its primacy. In such situations, other parts of the organization, even those with valuable information or perspectives to add, aren't consulted or, in the worst case, may be pushed out of the decision-making process. The result is that too narrow a focus is brought to bear on the issue and potential problems go unrecognized or are given too low a priority. To avoid recognition failures, leaders must strive to mitigate the impact of biases and ensure that organizational resources are appropriately allocated. One way to determine whether a recognition failure occurred is to assess whether leaders marshaled adequate resources to scan the environment for emerging threats. That means determining whether leaders did a reasonable job of directing the organization to gather, integrate, analyze, and interpret available data. Did the leader conduct an ongoing scan of those elements of the external operating environment on which the agency is most dependent or to which it is most vulnerable? Did the leader strive to integrate and analyze information from multiple sources to produce insights that can be acted upon? If the leaders did not do an adequate job, the organization's systems for recognizing emerging threats must be strengthened and the leaders' responsibility for crisis avoidance must be clarified and reinforced.

Prioritization Failures

Predictable surprises also occur when threats are recognized, but prevention is not given appropriate priority. Failures of prioritization are commonplace and result from cognitive, organizational, and political factors. Individuals may inappropriately discount the future, organizations may inadequately assess the likelihood of potentially damaging events, and special-interest groups may attempt to distort perceptions of potential costs and benefits to protect their perquisites.

Competing Priorities. How can leaders prioritize emerging threats when they are beset by competing demands on their attention? How can they possibly distinguish the surprise that will happen from the myriad potential surprises that won't? Of course, they can't make such distinctions with 100 percent accuracy. Uncertainty always exists—high-probability disasters sometimes do not occur, and low-probability ones sometimes do. Therefore, if an organization undertakes careful cost-benefit analyses and gives priority to those threats that would inflict the highest costs, its leaders should not be held accountable for a failure of prioritization. If the leaders fail to take these steps, they must concentrate on strengthening systems for setting priorities.

Overload. Those responsible for scanning the environment can also suffer from information overload, which keeps them from responding to all serious potential threats. As a result, their efforts either become too diffuse to be useful, or they are forced to ignore lower-priority areas. In either case, the organization risks failing to see an emerging threat until it is too late. Overload can occur when the resources devoted to environmental scanning are insufficient for the volume of information to be processed, or when the range of environmental sources of information increases over time without accompanying increases in scanning resources. Experienced managers will recognize selective attention, noise, and overload as the common state of most organizations. But the critical lesson for new leaders is that a failure to establish an ongoing process of environmental scanning will almost surely at some point result in the unpleasantness of a predictable surprise.

Secrecy. For government organizations engaged in national security, law enforcement, health issues, and the like, secrecy is necessary due to various security classifications and privacy concerns. But often the impulse toward secrecy extends to far less sensitive information because of tradition or misguided coveting of a valuable resource by those who see it as a source of influence. The net result is that important information is not shared internally, and even top leaders can remain uninformed. This trap offers a key lesson for new managers: when you are developing strategy, do not cut yourself off from consultation with those who you believe have potentially valuable input. To ward off a predictable surprise, you must temper your natural optimism with a thorough examination of all potential obstacles.

Conflicts of Interest. Conflicts of interest that result in poor prioritization are a major issue of concern for government organizations. Myriad layers of controls have been implemented to address such conflicts, from annual financial disclosure requirements to regular audits, to rigid ethics rules and criminal statutes governing who you may work for and what kind of access you are allowed to your former employer after leaving government service. Such transparency is not perfect—there are many loopholes—but overall it serves as a strong deterrent to corruption in carrying out a government leader's public-service responsibilities.

Discounting the Future. Predictable surprises often play out over time frames substantially longer than the expected tenure of many organizational leaders, especially those who serve in politically appointed positions that oversee the operations of ongoing government functions. This can create a variation of the free-rider problem. "Why," such a leader might ask, "should I be the one to grapple with this problem and take the heat when nothing is likely to go wrong during my watch? Better to focus on my short-term goals and reap rewards for their attainment."

Low-Probability Events. A related problem concerns dealing *wild cards*—potential problems that have low probabilities but very high costs. If terrorists could detonate a nuclear device (not necessarily a fission or fusion weapon; a radiological device would do) in a major city, it could do hundreds of billions—even trillions—of dollars of damage to the world economy. In theory, governments should allocate resources to avoiding a disaster like that—for example, by helping gather up more unsecured nuclear materials in the former Soviet Union or interdicting global trade in nuclear materials—based on a combined assessment of the likelihood of and the cost of such an event. In practice, however, government tends to underinvest in preventing wild-card events because the best intelligence and technical analyses available deem them as unlikely to occur, even though the potential impact would be catastrophic. On the other hand, governments often tend to overinvest in politically sensitive but less threatening crises, such as swine flu inoculations.

To avoid prioritization failures, leaders must strive to employ systematic and disciplined processes for establishing priorities. Tools such as decision analysis and risk analysis can help focus attention on issues that have a low likelihood but high consequences. Leaders must also be systematic in auditing their organization's incentive systems to ensure that conflicts of interest are not blocking action on emerging threats. Finally, leaders must lead organizational assessment and dialogue processes that focus attention on critical priorities.

Mobilization Failures

When an emerging threat has been determined to have serious potential consequences, leaders must mobilize to prevent it. This means marshaling support, educating important external constituencies, focusing the attention of key people in the organization, and making surprise prevention a personal priority. Organizational and political barriers often impede leaders' efforts to catalyze an adaptive response to emerging problems. Organizational inertia and complexity often erect major barriers to timely action. The actions of special-interest groups to delay or block action likewise can prevent leaders from addressing emerging threats until they explode into full-blown crises.

Collective Action Problems. One class of incentive failures that arises in all types of organizations and can create predictable surprises is known as *collective action problems*. For example, an agency's incentive awards plan may in fact create unhealthy internal competition between functions that draw on the same information resources, perhaps leading one to prevent the release of information to the other. Also, there are situations where members of an organization either try to take a "free ride" in the hope that others will assume responsibility for emerging problems, or to behave as if someone else were in charge of heading off looming problems. In both cases, no one feels compelled to act. This situation can become particularly dangerous when organizational members perceive that taking perhaps risky preventative action will yield them little reward if they are right and significant penalties if they are wrong.

Special-Interest Groups. Efforts to address pressing problems often yield broad, but modest, gains for many and large and painful costs for special interests. The result? Special interests are strongly motivated to block action, and the many who stand to benefit are more difficult to energize. Too often in these cases, disaster has to happen before the blocking power of special interest can be overcome.

Sometimes it is impossible to overcome opposition, even opposition that is likely to result in disaster. But the leader does have tools at his or her disposal to mobilize support to prevent predictable surprises. The most important of these is the courage to commit him- or herself to addressing looming disasters and the associated willingness to spend political capital to achieve this goal. Leaders also can employ the tools of strategic coalition building to analyze potential support and opposition and to build winning alliances in support of action. If leaders embrace the challenge of mobilization and exert effort commensurate with the risks involved, they should not be held accountable if a surprise occurs. If they fail to take preventive action, they must strengthen their capacity for mobilizing effective responses.

Learn-and-Disseminate Failures

Organizations suffer learn-and-disseminate failures when they fail to focus attention on learning from experience, embedding these lessons within the organization, and preventing their employees from forgetting. Once again, failures can occur in each of these key LD loop subprocesses and contribute to predictable surprises.

Focus Failures

Organizations fail to learn from past mistakes because they lack the mechanisms needed to share and codify, to the greatest extent possible, key lessons learned. Overcoming this tendency means setting up groups to analyze crisis experiences and generate lessons learned. Too often, however, organizations don't take those steps. Sometimes a leader who simply doesn't recognize the importance of learning from experiences is to blame. More often, however, responsibility lies with the organization, which is caught in a vicious cycle of firefighting and is too busy dealing with current crises to learn from past ones. Such circumstances set the stage for predictable surprises.

To avoid this problem, leaders must find ways to carve out the time and other resources necessary to invest in learning from experience. In a cost-constrained environment, investment in learning is too often the first thing to be jettisoned, so leaders must be prepared to fight hard for the organizational "slack" necessary for effective learning to occur.

Embedding Failures

Even when leaders focus attention on capturing lessons learned, the organization may still fail to disseminate the lessons appropriately, especially to the front lines. As a result, the benefits of experience do not get embedded into the organization's sense-and-respond systems, setting the stage for a future repetition of problems the organization already has confronted.

To understand why dissemination may not occur, it's important to distinguish between individual knowledge and relational knowledge, as well as between tacit knowledge and explicit knowledge. The four types of organizational knowledge are summarized in table 8-1.

The implications for the creation and preservation of organizational knowledge are far-reaching:

- *Tacit knowledge* gained by an individual who has confronted a problem is more difficult for an organization to capture than explicit knowledge. Think of employees responsible for maintaining a complex information system: they come to know all the system's idiosyncrasies, but that knowledge is very difficult to codify and transmit.

- *Relational knowledge* gained by a group confronting a problem is more difficult to capture than individual expertise. When faced with a crisis, for example, experienced teams know which members are going to perform which tasks and who is going to react in which ways; they don't have to consult procedures to mount a quick and effective response. That knowledge is difficult to capture.

TABLE 8-1

Types of organizational knowledge

	Individual knowledge (Possessed by individuals about how to do their jobs)	Relational knowledge (How to work effectively as a group)
Explicit knowledge: Transferable verbally or through writing	• Rules • Laws • Procedures • The "science" of a profession	• Organizational charts • Formal decision-making processes • Plans for coordination • Written communication protocols
Tacit knowledge: Transferable by being taught or working with someone who has experience	• Rules of thumb • Techniques • Approaches to individual decision making and problem solving • The "art" of a profession	• Approaches to group decision making and problem solving • Negotiated divisions of responsibility • Key sources of information and influence • Trust and credibility

- *Tacit-relational knowledge*—the knowledge that individuals have but cannot easily articulate to others—is the glue that holds the organization together and is by far the most difficult type to preserve.

To avoid dissemination failures, leaders must ensure that organizations match dissemination mechanisms to the type of knowledge to be preserved. Explicit lessons can be taught to individuals in the form of cause-and-effects models and rules of thumb, or they may be codified into more formal guidelines, checklists, regulations, and policies. More tacit and relational knowledge often must be transferred in the minds and hearts of people.

Forgetting Failures

Too many organizations fail to remember lessons from the past. This often occurs with the loss of people, including a new leader's predecessor, who may have taken away a valuable bank of knowledge. If possible, consultation with the person who held your job before you can be a valuable early learning experience and a good way to get a head start on avoiding a predictable surprise.

Fortunately, organizational memory typically contains significant redundancy. In a given unit, it is rare for all experienced personnel to depart at the same time, and those who remain can help educate new members. At the same time, the erosion of capability in critical areas can be subtle and all the more pernicious when it goes unnoticed. Costly and unnecessary memory loss afflicts most organizations. Any time there is a significant change in personnel, important knowledge can by irretrievably lost. Similarly, any time that responsibility for a critical activity, such as the start-up of a new program, is transferred from one part of the organization to another, critical insights can fall through the cracks. Leaders, therefore, must make knowledge preservation a core activity. This means identifying when key transfers of personnel and responsibility occur in the organization and intervening to assure that the thorough and accurate transfer of knowledge is high on the agenda.

Avoiding Transition Surprises

As a new leader, you are particularly at risk of being predictably surprised. In part, this is because you lack critical information and key relationships that help you spot emerging programs. The organization you are entering may also be overly siloed or have incentives problems or learning disabilities that further increase your vulnerability. Or there may be entrenched special interests that will fight to block needed change from occurring.

While these organizational risk factors are unquestionably problematic, the greatest risks may lie in how you approach your new leadership role. You may be susceptible because you have a particular mind-set that leads you to see some things and not others, and to gravitate toward certain problems and avoid others. What can you do to avoid being predictably surprised? The answers are easy to list but hard to realize:

- Discipline yourself to look in areas and ways that are not your preferences. This means forcing yourself to move out of your comfort zone. If you have a particular functional background, for example, there is the risk that you will view all problems through the lens of its mental models. To a person with a hammer, everything looks like a nail.

- Build a team with complementary skills. It is all too easy to staff your core team with people just like you. It's a natural impulse because it's easy and comfortable to surround yourself with people who think the way you do. Strive to get more cognitive and stylistic diversity on your team and do the hard work to integrate it. Also don't forget to explicitly task your staff with checking for predictable surprises lurking in their functions.

- Embed early-warning systems directly into the frontline processes of your organization. It can be tempting to treat sense-and-respond and learn-and-disseminate systems as add-ons. For example, some organizations set up units explicitly tasked to scan the external environment. While potentially helpful for integrating information and insight, such systems only work if sensing and learning are embedded at a more micro-level in the organization, where information about emerging problems will first become available. People at the front line need to be clear about what to do with such information and, critically, must be incentivized to share and not conceal it.

Conclusion

The failures in organizations' sense-and-respond and learn-and-disseminate loops described in this chapter are key contributors to predictable surprises. A weakness in any link in this sentinel chain of information processing—for Carrie's agency it was the SR loop—renders an organization, and its leaders, vulnerable. The types of failure also often compound and reinforce each other. Learning failures, for example, can result from a lack of integration, or from a lack of incentives among the organization's leaders to invest in capturing lessons learned. But in any case, leaders, especially those new to their positions, must be acutely aware that predictable surprises are awaiting them if they do not take effective action to neutralize their potential. There likely will be enough legitimate surprises during your tenure; work to deter the predictable ones by following the advice in this chapter.

ACCELERATION CHECKLIST

1. Are there areas of your organization that might harbor potential surprises? If so, what will you do to assess the risks?

2. Is the organization vulnerable to recognition failures? If so, what can you do to better recognize potential threats?

3. Do the organization's systems for planning and prioritization do a good job of assessing risk and setting priorities? If not, what can you do to strengthen prioritization?

4. Are there barriers to mobilizing responses to avert potential crises? If so, what can you do to mobilize resources and build coalitions?

5. Does the organization do a good job of focusing attention on learning, distilling lessons learned, and embedding them in sense-and-respond systems? If not, what can you do to enhance organizational learning?

6. Is the organization at risk due to memory loss? If so, what can you do to prevent or slow forgetting?

9

Manage Yourself

S HAWN WILLIAMS found himself facing an unanticipated challenge just two months after taking on an
assignment as director of a new organization established to implement the provisions of a recently enacted program
to improve drug-manufacturing safety. Essentially a start-up, the
new organization was not only operating in a politically and legally
sensitive environment, but it had a high public profile as well.
Shawn had established himself as an aggressive leader in his previous positions and now was eager to show quick results; he dove
into the task at hand with high energy and a sense of urgency.

By the end of just his first month on the job, he had established a
set of priorities for the organization, made key personnel appoint-
ments, and testified before two legislative committees. He also began a program of town hall–type appearances before interest groups
where he endeavored to articulate the organization's mission and
assure key constituencies about the impact of his program on the
availability and cost of new drugs.

Soon, however, Shawn began to get bogged down in myriad administrative matters involving internal budgeting, IT procurements, personnel issues, and acquiring needed office space. Even as pressure on
his time grew, he remained reluctant to delegate many of these matters and instead tried to juggle everything at once. In short order,
some of his highest-priority initiatives began to stall, as subordinates

had to queue up to get Shawn's OK before moving ahead. At the same time, Shawn's public appearances had heightened media interest in his proposals. Some of his remarks made under confrontational questioning by town-hall participants—especially his optimistic estimates of the time required to implement the program's provisions—had ignited a hostile political reaction by the administration's political opponents.

As he entered his third month, Shawn began to realize that, despite his best intentions, he had made too many independent promises and had undertaken too many initiatives at once. He had not taken the time to establish an organizational operating system that could accommodate all that needed to be done. His failure to seek advice and counsel from a number of trusted colleagues both inside and outside the organization only deepened the chaotic spiral he was being sucked into.

So, he stepped back, reassessed the way he was leading, and—now in conjunction with his direct reports and his bosses—developed a more systematic, team-based approach to implementing the new program, one with better focus on priority issues and challenging but reasonable timetables. The changes he introduced included weekly meetings with his direct reports, during which he was briefed on their respective administrative responsibilities and challenges and offered to get involved only when a problem clearly needed him to step in. Furthermore, he had given his direct reports discretionary spending authority that required his approval only for major expenditures. By relying more on his direct reports to oversee the administrative side of the organization, Shawn had more time to pursue his chief priority of introducing the public to the new organization.

Avoiding Common Traps

The life of a leader is always a balancing act, but never more so than during a transition. The uncertainty and ambiguity can be daunting; often, you don't even know what you don't know. Amid all this turmoil, you are expected to get acclimated quickly and begin to make positive changes in your new organization. For these reasons, keeping your balance is a key transition challenge.

Our research on failed transitions suggests that there are some common traps into which new leaders fall. Each of them enmeshes you in a *vicious cycle*, a self-reinforcing dynamic from which it will be difficult to escape. It is, therefore, imperative that you, like Shawn, are able to recognize when you are at risk and to take corrective actions. The seven most common traps include:

1. **Diffusion.** You can't hope to focus others if you can't focus yourself. There are an infinite number of tasks you could do during your transition, but only some are vital. Perhaps you may overestimate your ability to keep all the balls in the air. Every new leader has to do some parallel processing. But in doing so it is easy to reach a point of mental lockup, where you find yourself pulled from task to task faster than you can refocus on each new one. If important problems begin to go unaddressed, they can explode and consume more and more of your time. The result is a vicious cycle of firefighting.

2. **Undefended boundaries.** If you fail to establish clear boundaries that define what you are and are not willing to do, the people around you—bosses, peers, subordinates—will take whatever you have to give. The more you give, the less you will be respected and the more will be asked of you. If you cannot establish boundaries for yourself, you cannot expect others to do it for you.

3. **Brittleness.** The uncertainties inherent to transitions can breed rigidity and defensiveness, especially in new leaders with a high need for control. The likely result? Overcommitment to a failing course of action. You may make a call prematurely and then feel unable to back away from it without losing credibility. The longer you wait, the harder it is to admit you were wrong and the more calamitous the consequences. Or perhaps you decide that your way of accomplishing a particular goal is the only way. As a result, your

rigidity disempowers people who have equally valid ideas
about how to achieve the same goal.

4. **Isolation.** To be effective in the public sector, you have to
   be connected to the people who make action happen and
   to the subterranean flow of information, both of which can
   change quite quickly and frequently. It is surprisingly easy
   for new leaders to wind up isolated because they either over-
   rely on a few people or on official information for feedback
   and insight. Isolation also happens because you unintentionally discourage critical feedback or you are seen as
   being captured by competing interests. Whatever the reason, isolation breeds uninformed decision making, damaging your credibility and further reinforcing your isolation.
   Isolation in the public sector can also put a new leader at
   risk for leading with a mandate that is no longer supported
   at the top. It is important, therefore, for public-sector leaders to reestablish their mandates with any major leadership
   changes in positions above them.

5. **Biased judgment.** Biased judgment can take many forms.
   Overcommitment to a failing course of action because of ego
   and credibility issues is one version. Others include *confirmation bias,* the tendency to focus on information that confirms
   your beliefs and filters out what does not; *self-serving illusions,*
   a tendency to let your personal stake in a situation cloud
   your judgment; and *optimistic overconfidence,* or an under-
   estimation of the difficulties associated with your preferred
   course of action. Vulnerability to these biases is a constant,
   but you may be particularly at risk when the stakes grow,
   uncertainty and ambiguity increase, and emotions run high.

6. **Work avoidance.** You may have to make difficult decisions
   early in your tenure, perhaps on personnel or budgetary
   matters or on how to remedy a controversial issue. Consciously or unconsciously, you may choose to delay such

FIGURE 9-1

Yerkes-Dodson stress-performance curve

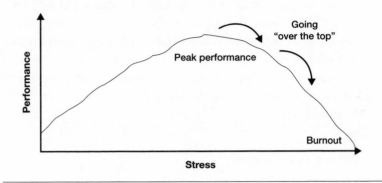

decisions by addressing other, more comfortable, issues instead—that is, falling into "work avoidance." The trap, of course, is that it only makes tough issues tougher.

7. **Overload.** Each of these traps can generate dangerous levels of stress. But not all stress is bad; there is a well-documented relationship between stress and performance known as the Yerkes-Dodson curve.[1] Whether stress is self-generated or externally caused, you need some—in the form of positive incentives or the consequences of inaction—to be productive. As illustrated in figure 9-1, your performance improves as you stress increases, at least at first. Then you reach a point, which varies from person to person, at which further demands, in the form of too many balls to juggle or too heavy an emotional load, begin to undermine your performance. This dynamic only increases the stress, reducing your performance level and creating a vicious cycle as you experience stress overload. You, like Shawn Williams, will find yourself working harder and achieving less.

Gauging Your Reaction to Stress

Before proceeding further, take a few minutes and complete the assessment shown in table 9-1. For each statement, circle the response that best represents your reactions to stress. Think about periods in the past when you have experienced extreme personal or professional stress. What were your characteristic reactions in such situations? If you have someone you trust and who knows you well, make a copy of the assessment and have him or her do an assessment of you too.

Assessing Your Reactions

The assessment is designed to give you scores on three stress-related indexes:

- **Physical.** The impact of stress on your physical well-being.

- **Cognitive.** The impact of stress on your ability to think.

- **Emotional.** The impact of stress on your emotional state.

Follow the instructions in table 9-2 to calculate your three scores.

Now take a look at these scores. Lower scores are better. In which of these three areas are you most affected by stress? Is the overall impact of stress on you 2.5 or greater? If so, you may be at risk for stress-related degradation of your performance.

Assessing Your Coping Behaviors

The diagnostic also gives you a score for your *coping behaviors:* the things you do to release or deal with stress. Follow the instructions in table 9-3 to calculate your score for coping behaviors:

Once again, a lower score is better.

Finally, take some time to think about how you could better identify when stress is becoming too great and what you can do to alleviate it.

TABLE 9-1

Stress assessment

Do not turn the page before completing the table.

When I am under great stress, I . . .

1 = Strongly disagree	4 = Agree
2 = Disagree	5 = Strongly agree
3 = Neither agree nor disagree	

1. Have more difficulty sleeping.	1	2	3	4	5
2. Feel sharper mentally.	1	2	3	4	5
3. Become more domineering.	1	2	3	4	5
4. Suffer more aches and pains.	1	2	3	4	5
5. Pay more attention to personal relationships.	1	2	3	4	5
6. Become more forgetful.	1	2	3	4	5
7. Feel more isolated.	1	2	3	4	5
8. Feel very focused.	1	2	3	4	5
9. Eat more than usual.	1	2	3	4	5
10. Feel paralyzed by indecision.	1	2	3	4	5
11. Become more judgmental.	1	2	3	4	5
12. Pay less attention to personal grooming.	1	2	3	4	5
13. Feel more energized.	1	2	3	4	5
14. Act more impulsively.	1	2	3	4	5
15. Get "down" more easily.	1	2	3	4	5
16. Exercise more frequently.	1	2	3	4	5
17. Become more patient with others.	1	2	3	4	5
18. Have more difficulty concentrating.	1	2	3	4	5
19. Turn to friends for support.	1	2	3	4	5
20. Feel more anxious.	1	2	3	4	5
21. Get tired more easily.	1	2	3	4	5
22. Drink more than usual.	1	2	3	4	5

TABLE 9-2

Calculating your stress level

	How to calculate	Your score
Physical	Add your scores for questions #1, #4, #12, and #21. Subtract your score for question #13. Then add 6 and divide the result by 5.	
Cognitive	Add your scores for questions #6, #11, #14, and #18. Subtract your scores for questions #2 and #8. Then add 12 and divide the result by 6.	
Emotional	Add your scores for questions #3, #7, #10, #15, and #20. Subtract your score for question #17. Then add 6 and divide the result by 6.	
Overall impact	Add your scores for physical, cognitive, and emotional as calculated above and divide by 3.	

TABLE 9-3

Scoring your coping behaviors

	How to calculate	Your score
Coping behaviors	Add your scores for questions #9 and #22. Subtract your scores for questions #5, #16, and #19. Then add 18 and divide the result by 5.	

The Four Pillars of Self-Efficacy

How can you avoid these traps? Instead of creating vicious cycles, how can you create *virtuous cycles* that build momentum rather than sap your strength? We will call the equilibrium you should aim for *self-efficacy,* a state that is built on a foundation of these four pillars:

1. Adoption of the *transition success strategies* presented in the previous eight chapters

2. Self-awareness concerning your style and its match to the situation, and the use of *complementary teams* for dealing with mismatches

3. Enforcement of some *personal disciplines* that increase your efficacy

4. Creation and use of *support systems,* at work and elsewhere, which help you maintain your equilibrium

Pillar 1: Transition Success Strategies

The strategies spelled out in the previous eight chapters represent a template for how to learn, set priorities, create plans, and direct actions to build momentum. As you see these strategies work and achieve some early successes, you will feel more confident and energized by what you are accomplishing. As you progress through your transition, think about the challenges you are facing in light of the core challenges summarized in table 9-4, and identify chapters to which you want to return.

Pillar 2: Complementary Teams

Why do leaders fail to make successful transitions? Many misdiagnose their situations. But new leaders can understand the situations they face and still fail because their style is a poor match for the situation and the type of organization they are in. Shawn Williams's lone ranger approach in a start-up organization operating in a highly participative and consultative environment damaged his credibility early on. If he had been leading a law-enforcement organization that required fast action, a highly participative leadership style could have been equally as damaging. You must, therefore, understand your style, its match to the situation and organization as a whole, and the potential vulnerabilities that result. Only then can you take action to compensate for them.

Style consists of the distinctive ways you tend to make sense of the world and interact with others in leadership roles. Important dimensions of your leadership style include how you prefer to:

- Learn in new situations

- Communicate with others

TABLE 9-4

Transition strategies

Core challenge	Diagnostic questions
Clarify expectations	Are you figuring out what is expected of you? Are you engaging your boss in conversations about situation, expectations, style, resources, and personal development?
Match strategy to situation	Are you diagnosing the type of transition you are facing and the implications for what to do and what not to do?
Accelerate your learning	Are you figuring out what you need to learn, from whom to learn it, and how to speed up the learning process?
Secure early wins	Are you focusing on the vital priorities that advance long-term goals and build short-term momentum?
Build your team	Are you assessing, restructuring, and aligning your team to leverage what you are trying to accomplish?
Create alliances	Are you building a base of internal and external support for your initiatives so you are not pushing rocks uphill?
Achieve alignment	Are you identifying and fixing frustrating misalignments of strategy, structure, systems, and skills?
Avoid predictable surprises	Are you taking measures to identify and therefore avoid and or respond quickly to predictable surprises?

- Influence and be influenced

- Make important decisions

Style doesn't reflect your capabilities. Rather, it reflects your preferences. Your preferences are in part in-born and in part the result of your personal and professional experiences. Different styles can be effective at certain times and in particular situations. You likely have a preferred style that you feel most comfortable with. By understanding your preferred leadership style, you can figure out when to use it most effectively—and when you might be better off employing a different approach.

There are basically four areas of leadership style—learning, communicating, influencing, and decision-making. Each has a range of behaviors associated with it. You will likely lean toward one end of the spectrum for each. Take a look at "Diagnosing Your Leadership Style" for some insight into your preferences.

Diagnosing Your Leadership Style

Learning style—How do you prefer to learn and gather information?

- *Do you prefer to learn by gathering hard data (numbers, facts, figures) and then analyzing the results—or by gathering soft data (expert judgments, opinions)?* The advantage of the hard-data approach is that numbers can give firmer information than intuition or stories can. The disadvantage is that problems often have political or cultural origins—which have little to do with hard data.

Communication style—How do you communicate with direct reports, and how do you prefer that they communicate with you?

- *Do you have an open-door policy, where anyone can come in with a question or comment at any time?* If so, the advantage is that your employees will feel that they can make their opinions heard. Thus, you may get more honest information. The disadvantage is that, with too many people interrupting you during the day, you may not have time to get other work done.

- *Would you rather receive information in writing and e-mail or through conversation (including voice mail)?* The advantages of writing and e-mail are that you can read messages when you choose and keep a record of each communication. The disadvantage is that direct reports could feel distant from you.

- *Do you prefer to talk with people individually or in groups to gather information and opinions?* Individual conversations can

---

be revealing but time consuming. Talking in groups can be more efficient, but it also can generate less detailed information.

Influence style—How do you influence or motivate your direct reports?

- *Do you prefer the push approach (influencing others by setting goals, measuring performance, and offering incentives), or would you rather pull people along (by creating a vision and inspiring teamwork)?* The push style rests on the belief that concrete incentives (rewards and punishments) are what motivate employees. The approach sets clear expectations and tangible rewards and can work well when executed fairly. The risk is that employees will do only whatever is necessary to attain the reward— and no more. At the same time, developing a compelling vision takes considerable effort, and not everyone responds to pull.

Decision-making style—How do you tend to make important decisions?

- *Do you consult with direct reports and then make the call yourself, or do you seek to build consensus within your group to gain their support during implementation?* The consult-and-decide approach can be effective as long as employees feel that you're taking their voices into account in your decision. But if they feel as though they have no voice, they may not support you in the decision-implementation phase. The build-consensus approach may work best if it's important to gain the acceptance of those most affected by your decision, but it can sometimes take too much time to be feasible.

Different leadership styles have associated strengths and weaknesses that vary with the ST$_A$RS situation you face. In turnarounds, for example, a hard-data and experiential learning style can be a good match. You have to diagnose the fundamentals quickly but can afford to make some small mistakes. The same learning style, however, can be a bad match for a sustaining-success situation, where much of what you need to learn concerns culture and politics, and where an experiential approach can make you look undisciplined and even dangerous.

A consult-and-decide decision-making style is likewise a good match for start-up situations, where the key is to create some direction and get the foundations in place. But it could be disastrous to adopt the same style in a realignment situation, where the key is to move people from denial to awareness of the need for change. Efforts on your part to make the call on key issues can easily backfire by stimulating the organization's immune system and unnecessarily stiffening resistance.

To avoid potential problems, you need to know when and how to adjust your style to fit a particular situation. The starting point for doing this is self-awareness about your style and its associated strengths and weaknesses. You then can combine this awareness with your diagnosis of the situation—using the ST_ARS model—to identify potential vulnerabilities.

What do you do if your style is not a good match for the situation? There are essentially two ways to compensate. First, you can act against your preferences—focusing hard on resisting your preferential ways of doing things. If you prefer to make decisions through consensus building but are entering a turnaround situation, you should bias yourself in the direction of consult-and-decide. Second, you can put together a team that includes people with styles that are a better match to the situation. If you are in a sustaining-success situation and you have a hard-data, experiential learning style, for example, you would be well advised to have people on your team with soft-data and conceptual learning styles.

Pillar 3: Personal Disciplines

Knowing what you should be doing is not the same as doing it. Ultimately, success or failure emerges from the accumulation of daily choices that either propel you in productive directions or move you down the wrong path. This is the territory of the third pillar of personal efficacy: personal disciplines.

Personal disciplines are the regular routines that you enforce on yourself. The specific disciplines you choose to develop depend on your strengths and weaknesses. Though you may have a great deal of insight into yourself, you should also consult others who know you well and whom you trust. Some 360-degree feedback can be useful for learning what others see as your strengths and—importantly— your potential weak spots.

Here are some disciplines to stimulate your thinking about routines you need to develop.

Plan to Plan. Do you devote time daily and weekly to a plan-work-evaluate cycle? If not, or if you do so irregularly, you need to be more disciplined about planning. At the end of each day, spend ten minutes evaluating how well you met the goals you set the previous day and planning for the next day. Get into the habit of doing this. Even if you fall behind, you will be more in control.

Judiciously Defer Commitment. Do you often make commitments on the spur of the moment and regret them later? If so, you must learn to defer commitment. When pressed to make a commitment that you are uncertain of, begin with saying, "Let me think about it and get back to you." If pressed for an immediate answer, say, "If I have to decide now, then I must say no. But if you can wait a bit, I'll give it more thought." Begin with no, as it is easier and less damaging to your credibility than saying yes and then changing your mind. Ask yourself whether the "future you" will be unhappy with the "present you" for saying yes. If the answer is yes, then decline the commitment.

Set Aside Time for the Real Work. Do you devote time each day to the most important work that needs to be done? It is easy to get caught up in the flow of transactions—phone calls, meetings, e-mails—and never find the time to focus on the medium term, let alone the long run. If you are having trouble getting the real work done, discipline yourself to set aside a particular time each day, even if it's only thirty minutes, when you close the door, shut off the phone, and ignore e-mail so you can focus, focus, focus.

Go to the Balcony. Do you find yourself getting too caught up in the emotional dimension of difficult situations? If so, discipline yourself to step back and take another look at the big picture before reinserting yourself. Prominent authorities in the fields of leadership and negotiation have long praised the value of "going to the balcony" in this way.[2] It can be tough to do when stakes and emotions are running high and you are emotionally involved, but with practice it is a valuable skill that you can cultivate.

Focus on Process. Do your good ideas often run into roadblocks with others? Does the way you make decisions seem to cause unnecessary dissent and disagreement? If so, discipline yourself to focus on *process* before plunging ahead. How are others likely to react to your ideas? How might you manage the process of consultation and decision making to increase your effectiveness? Remember: people will often go along with things they are not completely happy with if they perceive the process as fair.[3]

Check In with Yourself. Are you as aware as you need to be of your reactions to events during your transition? If not, discipline yourself to engage in structured reflection about your situation. For some, this means simply jotting down a few thoughts, impressions, and questions at the end of each day. For others, it means setting aside time each week to assess how things are going. Find an approach that suits your style, and discipline yourself to use it regularly. Work to translate the resulting insights into action. Consider adopting the guidelines for self-reflection listed in the box "Guidelines for Structured Reflection."

Recognize When to Quit. Transitions are marathons, not sprints. If you find yourself approaching overload more than occasionally, you have to discipline yourself to know when to quit. This

Guidelines for Structured Reflection

The power of structured reflection is heightened if you pursue it regularly and are attentive to how your responses change over time. Consider setting aside fifteen minutes at the end of each week to answer the same set of questions. Save your responses so you can look back regularly at the preceding couple of weeks. You will see patterns develop, both in the nature of the problems you face and in your reactions to them.

What do you feel so far? On a scale of high to low, do you feel:

- Excited? If not, why not? What can you do about it?

- Confident? If not, why not? What can you do about it?

- In control of your success? What can you do about it?

What has bothered you so far?

- With whom have you failed to connect? Why?

- Of the meetings you have attended, which has been the most troubling? Why?

- Of all that you have seen or heard, what has disturbed you most? What has gone well and poorly?

- Which interactions would you handle differently if you could? Which exceeded your expectations? Why?

- Which of your decisions have turned out particularly well? Not so well? Why?

- What missed opportunities do you regret most? Was a better result blocked primarily by you or by something beyond your control?

Now focus on the biggest challenges or difficulties you are facing. Be honest with yourself. Are your difficulties situational, or do their sources lie within you? Even experienced and skilled people blame problems on the situation rather than on their own actions. The net effect is that they are less proactive than they could be.

is easy to say, but hard to do, of course, especially when you are facing a deadline and one hour might make the difference. It may, in the short run, but the long-run cost could be steep. Work hard at understanding when you are at the point of diminishing returns, and take a break—whatever refreshes you.

Pillar 4: Personal Support Systems

The fourth pillar of self-efficacy is personal support systems. This means asserting control in your local environment, stabilizing the home front if you are relocating, and building a solid advice-and-counsel network.

Assert Control Locally. It is hard to focus on work if the basic physical infrastructure that supports you is not in place. Even if you have more pressing worries, you must move quickly to set up your new office, develop routines, and, if applicable, clarify expectations with your new assistant, and so on. If necessary, assemble a set of temporary resources—files, references, information technology, and staff support—to tide you over until the permanent systems are operational.

Stabilize the Home Front. It is a fundamental rule of competition to avoid fighting on too may fronts. For new leaders with families, this means stabilizing the home front so you can devote the necessary attention to work. You cannot hope to create value at work if you are depleting value at home.

If your new position involves a relocation, your family is also in transition. Your spouse may have to make a job transition as well, and your children may have to change schools and leave friends. In other words, the fabric of your family's life may be disrupted just when you most need support and stability. The stresses of your transition can amplify the strain of your family's transition. Also, family members' difficulties can add to your already heavy emotional load, undermining your ability to create value and lengthening the time of your transition. So when a move is part of your transition, focus on accelerating the family's transition too. There is no avoiding disruption, but talking about it and working through the sense of loss together can be helpful.

Even if your new position does not involve a family move, the natural stress and time requirements of your new position may prove disruptive to family routines. When Mom or Dad is no longer regularly there in the morning or at dinnertime, when frequent travel is required, or when games and recitals are missed, it is natural for children to be unhappy with the change. Similarly, when one spouse is no longer able to carry an equal share of work at home, marital strains can appear. Whether the transition takes six months or a year, keeping communication lines open about the various changes it may be imposing on familiar family routines and coming up with ways to share the burden is essential to weathering this perhaps difficult time and emerging at the end of it in good shape as a family and as an individual. See "Accelerating Your Family's Transition" for some additional tips on how to speed your family's transition to a new location.

Build Your Advice-and-Counsel Network. No leader, no matter how capable and energetic, can do it all. Just ask Shawn Williams. You need a network of trusted advisers within and outside the organization whom you can talk with about what you are experiencing and, importantly, who will give you honest feedback about what you are doing. Your network is an indispensable resource that can help you avoid becoming isolated and losing perspective. As a starting point, you need to cultivate the three types of advice givers described in table 9-5: technical advisers, cultural interpreters, and political counselors.

You also need to think hard about the mix of internal and external advice givers you want to cultivate. Insiders know the organization and its culture and politics. Seek out people who are well connected and whom you can trust to help you grasp what is really going on. This is a priceless resource for any new leader, but especially so for the leader who is new to an agency.

Accelerating Your Family's Transition

- *Analyze your family's existing support system.* Moving severs your ties with all the people who provide essential services for your family: doctors, lawyers, dentists, babysitters, tutors, coaches, and more. It's important to recognize this early, do an inventory, identify priorities, and invest in finding replacements quickly.

- *Get your spouse back on track, too.* Your spouse may quit his or her old job with the intention of finding a new one after relocating. Unhappiness can fester if the search is slow. To accelerate it, negotiate up front with your company for job-search support, or find such support shortly after moving.

- *Time the family move carefully.* For children, it is substantially more difficult if they have to move in the middle of a school year. If possible, consider waiting until the end of school to move your family. The price for you, of course, is separation from your loved ones and the wear and tear of commuting.

- *Retain the familiar.* Reestablish familiar family rituals as quickly as possible, and maintain them throughout the transition. Help from favorite relatives, such as grandparents, also makes a difference.

At the same time, insiders cannot be expected to give you dispassionate or disinterested views of events. Thus, you should augment your internal network with outside advisers and counselors who will help you work through issues and decisions you are facing. They should be skilled at listening and asking questions, have good insights into the way organizations work well, and have your best interests at heart.

Use table 9-6 to assess your advice-and-counsel network. Analyze each person in terms of the domains in which they assist you and whether they are insiders or outsiders.

TABLE 9-5

Types of advice-givers

Type of supporters	Their roles	How they help you
Technical advisers	• Provide expert analysis of technologies and strategy.	• They suggest applications for new technologies. • They recommend strategies for implementation. • They provide timely and accurate information.
Cultural interpreters	• Help you understand the new culture and (if that is your objective) to adapt to it.	• They provide you with insight into cultural norms, mental models, and guiding assumptions. • They help you learn to speak the language of the new organization.
Internal political counselors	• Help you deal with political relationships within your new organization.	• They help you implement the advice of your technical advisors. • They serve as a sounding board as you think through options for implementing your agenda. • They challenge you with what-if questions.

Now go to the balcony. Will your existing network provide the support you need in your new situation? Don't assume that people who have been helpful before will necessarily be helpful in your new situation because you will be facing new kinds of problems. For example, the higher the level of responsibility of your new position, the stronger the need for a political counselor. (You also should be thinking ahead. Because it takes time to develop an effective network, it's not too early to focus on what sort of network you will need for your *next* job. How will your need for advice change?)

To develop an effective support network, you need to make sure that you have the right help and that your support network is there when you need it. Does your support network have the following qualities?

TABLE 9-6

Assessing your network

	Technical advisers	Cultural interpreters	Internal political counselors
Internal advisers and counselors *(Inside your new organization)*			
External advisers and counselors *(Outside your new organization)*			

- The right mix of technical advisers, cultural interpreters, and political counselors.

- The right mix of internal and external advice givers. You want honest feedback from insiders and the dispassionate prospective of outside observers.

- External supporters who are loyal to you as an individual, not to your organization or unit. Typically, these are long-standing colleagues and friends.

- Internal advisers who are trustworthy, whose personal agendas don't conflict with yours, and who offer straight and accurate advice.

- Representatives of key constituencies who can help you understand their perspectives. You do not want to restrict yourself to one or two points of view.

Finally, as you build your own support network, keep the following principles in mind:

- **Trusted friends aren't always the best counselors.** Don't assume that trusted friends will make competent political counselors or technical advisers. They may be loyal, but they don't necessarily have the specific skills needed to help you in your job.

- **Special competencies are not usually interchangeable.** Don't assume that a technical adviser can be an equally competent political counselor. Each type of supporter has special competencies that are usually not interchangeable.

- **Past advisers may not be able to help you in the future.** Don't assume that someone who has been helpful in the past will continue to be helpful in your new situation. You will encounter different problems, and a former adviser may not be able to help you in your new role.

Conclusion

You will have to fight to maintain your equilibrium throughout your transition. Shawn Williams, fortunately, caught himself fairly early in the process. Ultimately, your success or failure will flow from the many small choices you make along the way. These choices can create momentum—for the organization and for you—or they can result in death by a thousand cuts. Your day-to-day actions during your transition establish the pattern for all that follows, not just for the organization but also for your personal efficacy and your well-being.

ACCELERATION CHECKLIST

1. What is your style, and how good a match is it for the situation? What can you do to compensate for potential style-related vulnerabilities?

2. What personal disciplines do you most need to develop or improve? What can you do to gain more control over your local environment?

3. What personal support systems do you need to build?

4. What are your priorities for strengthening your advice-and-counsel network?

5. In which domains do you need most support: technical, political, or personal?

Conclusion:
Accelerate Everyone

THE STRATEGIES presented in the previous nine chapters should propel you on your way to getting up to speed *and* getting it right during your transition period. But an important question remains: why is it that so few organizations in the public sector pay so little real attention to this critical period in the careers of key employees upon whom they rely so heavily? Though there are public agencies that are exceptions to this rule, too often new leaders at all levels are largely left to their own resources to gain the learning and other critical assets they need to succeed.

One reason for this is the changing nature of senior leadership positions in many public-sector organizations at all levels of government. Flattened hierarchies and increased outsourcing have resulted in senior managers' spending more time managing sets of contractors than supervising their agency's employees. This leaves them with less time or incentive to develop and counsel their direct reports and other staff. As a result, those important leadership functions have migrated more and more to human resource professionals who, while well equipped to impart "hard" technical skills, cannot teach the valuable experience-born wisdom that can be transferred from mentoring senior managers to their less experienced counterparts. Particularly missing is the transfer of the "soft" skills, such as decision making and team building, needed to effectively take charge in a new role.

Another reason is the "leadership-development-through-Darwinian-evolution" culture that many organizations mistakenly employ as a test of a new manager's capability. Rather than aim to make available the kinds of support necessary during the new leader's transition period, organizations often leave these key people on their own to sink or swim. Sending promising managers into challenging situations unprepared is a flawed—and, in many ways, irresponsible—approach to leadership development. Remember that there are many different kinds of transitions, and the lessons learned in one type of transition may not transfer to the next organizational level or situation. The result of this approach is that some high-potential people fall into early transition traps and sink; others swim, but only by the happenstance of ending up in the right kind of position, or because they have the right lifeguard looking out for them.

In the course of our research for this book, we encountered leaders who had derived great personal and professional benefit from having worked under mentoring leaders early in their careers. Their recollections of the experience were remarkably similar: each believed that they had gained priceless knowledge and self-confidence from the opportunity afforded them by bosses who understood the value of sharing their wisdom and insights, and they were enduringly grateful for the support they received. Conversely, we also encountered leaders whose experiences with earlier bosses were not so constructive, and they too voiced similar recollections: they recalled feeling confused about what was expected of them, isolated from and uninformed about higher-level decisions that affected the operations they were assigned to lead, and generally unvalued as team members. Each of them eventually lost their motivation to excel and moved on to other positions as soon as they could do so.

The value of mentoring is clear. Where it is a standard practice of senior executives, newer leaders tend to excel and to reach the break-even point earlier. Where it is absent, motivation often lags and takes organizational performance down with it. The best organizations are meritocracies, where people compete and rise because they possess the talent, drive, and insight to prove themselves as capable leaders. But true meritocracies must start with a level playing field so that those who rise to leadership positions do so because they have the right stuff and not because they fit some predetermined profile or just happen to get placed in situations where their skills are well matched. Successful meritocracies require the direct involvement of senior managers in the development and acceleration of newer leaders. Organizations are not well served in the long run by unregulated Darwinian leadership development.

Creating a Common Language

You can accelerate *everyone* by institutionalizing the transition-management model presented in this book. If you and all new leaders in your organization use these success strategies, you will not just prevent predictable surprises and other kinds of failure; you will capture substantial gains in overall organizational performance. The faster everyone settles in, the faster the organization can begin to make the right moves to improve.

How might you go about introducing the transition-management framework in your organization? The starting point is to introduce a new language *within* the agency for talking about developing new leaders. This common language probably is the single most important step your organization will take to institutionalize transition acceleration. Imagine that every time a person assumed a new leadership role, he or she was able to talk with bosses, peers, and staff about the following elements of the transition-management framework:

- Their progress in engaging their boss in the five conversations about situation, expectations, style, resources, and personal development.

- The type of transition they are in, using ST_ARS terminology, and what that means for diagnosing the associated challenges and opportunities.

- Their agenda for technical, cultural, and political learning and the key elements of their learning plan.

- Their A item priorities, goals for behavioral change, and ideas where they might obtain early wins.

- Their priorities for strengthening their advice-and-counsel network.

A common language facilitates discussion of these issues and makes conversations dramatically more efficient. Perhaps more important, talking about these subjects means that conversations will happen that wouldn't have happened otherwise. In our discussion of coalition building, we illustrated the complexity of internal communications with an example of an influence map. Consider how much more efficient such communications could be if everyone on the map used the same terms. Using shared terminology also tends to make people more forthcoming, more likely to share personal experiences, and more tolerant of others' transition problems. This helps move the organization beyond the sink-or-swim mentality.

But anyone who ever has tried to introduce a new idea to an established organization will tell you that it is an uphill battle. The struggle is often even more difficult at the senior-most levels in a government agency because the short-term service of many political appointees who may oversee agency operations and to whom the senior executive may report impedes establishing over time the kind of dialogue needed to implement the framework. So begin locally, with people who work for you, those who are new as well as those who are not. And when you next hire people for a leadership position, experiment with how quickly you can bring them to the breakeven point. Start by introducing them to the five-conversation plan, and then have them diagnose the ST_ARS situation they face in their new role and discuss it with you. Merge this with the expectations conversation, and then work with them to create a learning agenda and plan. Help them identify people to reach out to and whose support they will need. Press them on their priorities and plans for securing early wins. Once the breakeven point is reached, urge them to employ the same approach with their staffs. Such a strategy brought success to Sandra Martin and Amy Donovan and would have helped Duane Robinson and Joe Raab equally, irrespective of the differences in their individual situations, by enlisting the efforts of their staffs to establish new performance goals.

In parallel with this, choose a direct report who has been around awhile and who you believe is open minded. Experiment with helping him or her accelerate his or her own staff. Put this person in the role of teacher, which is often the best way to learn something new. See how far down you can cascade the framework.

Working with a Team

If you are building a new team, consider using the ST_ARS framework to accelerate the team-building process. One virtue of this framework is that it supplies the team with a common language for talking about shared challenges. This can be especially powerful if your team mixes seasoned veterans with people who are transitioning into new roles. Furthermore, such a strategy ensures respect for the past and works to prevent falling into the lone ranger trap that got Kevin Cody and Shawn Williams into so much early trouble. By introducing a new framework and language, you level the playing field between the old guard and the new.

Start by providing your team with an overview of the transition-acceleration framework. Then focus the team on doing a shared situational analysis using the ST_ARS model. (Recall the approach employed by both Sandra Martin and Amy Donovan: facing a mix of ST_ARS situations, which is a problem common to many new leaders, they each took the time to familiarize themselves and then the people in their organizations with the true nature of the task ahead.) Push team members to clarify the key challenges and opportunities. Then move on to alignment issues—strategy, structure, systems, skills, and culture. Next work with the team to define goals and get some early wins. Finally, explore the kinds of coalitions you and the team will have to build to marshal the support you will need to advance key initiatives.

Bringing People In from Outside

Transition management is especially important when a new leader is brought into the organization from the outside. But few organizations do a good job of helping outsiders become insiders. As a result, promising people often make unnecessary mistakes, particularly in the areas of organizational culture and politics.

How do you avoid this? Start by using the ST_ARS model to identify the jobs that are best suited for outside hires. Don't let new leaders hired from outside the organization be set up for failure by putting them in a realignment situation (e.g., without adequate support and advice). Teach them the same transition-acceleration vocabulary that insiders speak so they can converse easily about, for example, what is considered a "win" in your organization. Develop a primer about the company culture, perhaps a video of leaders who have successfully transitioned in from the outside talking about what worked and what didn't.

Developing High-Potential Leaders

Effective systems for identifying and evaluating members of the organization who have high leadership potential call for (1) rigorous evaluation of leadership skills through such means as regular and thorough performance reviews, short-term leadership assignments with a task force or special project, and the use of a leadership assessment center where candidates are placed in simulated leadership situations and observed by experienced leaders who evaluate candidates' performance; and (2) thoughtful design of developmental pathways that identifies artificial barriers to advancement and broadens the candidate pools of potential leaders to include those who might not otherwise be considered because of their occupations or organizational locations.

When it comes to developing talent, an executive-development program based on the transition-acceleration model can be a central component of a more ambitious strategy for identifying and developing high-potential leaders within your agency. In such programs, which typically last days, cohorts of high-potential leaders who are transitioning into new roles are introduced to the transition-management model, work through new leader situations and case studies, and do some planning for their own transitions. In the course of intense small-group work, longer-term advice-and-counsel networks often coalesce.

There are many examples of outstanding leadership-development programs throughout the public sector, and we encountered many of them in our research. One important feature they all share is a strict adherence to equality of opportunity, not only as a legal and moral imperative but also as a means of broadening as much as possible the search for leadership potential. These programs also all feature cross-functional experience, regional assignments where appropriate, regular assessments of performance under a variety of conditions, and a combination of on-the-job and academic training opportunities. However, many other systems fell short in both evaluation and development because they lacked a framework for characterizing developmental assignments and, as a result, could not make the critical connection between executive-development strategy and organizational situation. Without such a framework, it is problematic to make comparisons between high-potential individuals placed in dissimilar situations. Many systems for identifying and nurturing leadership potential also lack a way of describing—and thus managing—the sequence of positions through which high-potential leaders progress.

These systems can be strengthened substantially by looking at the people *and* the transition situations, as defined by the ST_ARS model, they might have experienced. The ST_ARS model provides not only a basis for evaluating performance in different types of situations, but also a basis for charting the progression of high-potential leaders through a series of positions that build their capability to manage a broad range of situations. Preparing people to manage different types of organizational situations constitutes an additional facet of leadership development that complements analyses of (1) breadth of functional experience and (2) key passages between levels in the organization.

Accelerating Agency Integration

When agencies or their components combine, integration of the different cultures, political dynamics, and technologies involved presents serious challenges to the new organization's leaders. Much attention has been paid to the enormity of combining the vastly differing missions and cultures of the agencies that now compose the new federal Department of Homeland Security, the formation of which constitutes the grandest government reorganization in more than fifty years. On a smaller scale, recall the challenge faced by Amy Donovan as she strived to pool knowledge, resources, and best practices to improve the performance of three service centers with significantly different cultures.

In each of these cases, and the many other examples in between, the transition-acceleration model developed in this book can be used as a driver of agency integration. When organizations collide, the various pieces start out speaking somewhat different languages. Culture clashes often are as much about language as they are about values and expectations. Misunderstandings generate conflict, which only undermines the integration process. The transition-acceleration model provides a common language that all organizations can use and that can help avoid such conflict.

Moving Forward

We wrote this book because too many talented people in government have had to learn about transitions through hard-won—and sometimes very costly—personal experience. Given that there is so much cumulative wisdom about how to get up to speed more efficiently and effectively, this is terribly wasteful. Experience is what we gain by learning from our mistakes (and, of course, our successes). But too many new leaders have had to reinvent the wheel when they could have benefited from the experience of others. Mistakes have consequences beyond teaching lessons, consequences that include severe collateral damage to organizations and careers. It's for this reason that we set out to collect and synthesize the insight of leaders who have succeeded and failed in making significant transitions into new roles in government.

Competition for leadership positions in government has always been stiff. Reductions in available positions and increasing complexity of the challenges facing public-sector leaders have combined to make it even stiffer. For those who have attained or aspire to senior leadership positions, realizing your ambition will require ever more attention to your own personal development and care in planning to make successful transitions. Ambition is indispensable, but it won't be enough to take you where you want to go; that takes preparation. Every tier in public organizations presents its own unique set of challenges for new leaders. For those in middle to upper-middle management or senior specialist positions who aspire to the executive level, a key challenge is to plan your own development.

We all have heard the expression, "It's lonely at the top." But those who have served at the top usually once were at the bottom and the middle, and they will tell you that it's even lonelier there. It can be frustrating for an ambitious person in the lower or middle ranks, restricted by organizational structures from gaining insights into executive decision making, to observe the organization's top leaders and accurately discern their priorities and patterns of leadership behavior. Under such circumstances, planning your own development might seem to be a matter of guesswork. Nothing could be further from the truth. Given the intensity of competition you are likely to face, and the pressure to show results once you arrive at a leadership post, guessing at what is needed to succeed would be exactly the wrong way to go about preparing yourself. Instead, the existence of uncertainty and the high probability of change makes it even more important to go about your development plans in a carefully considered way.

This book provides practical guidance for how to do this. Following its recommendations will help you prepare and succeed as a leader in the public sector. As you read through the chapters, there may be times when you feel overwhelmed by the scope and detail of the information we present. Don't worry about it; we wrote the book not to be read *once*, but to be kept as a constant reference for planning your career and for succeeding in your ambitions for leadership. The cases and the guidance provided are based on research with outstanding leaders serving in many aspects of federal and state government who were eager to share their experiences with you. We hope you can make good use of their insights—excellent public leadership benefits our nation as well as all its citizens.

Notes

Introduction

1. This figure was derived by applying annual turnover rates to total numbers of supervisors and managers in federal, state, and local governments. The total number of employees in these sectors in 2004 was 29.5 million. Supervisors and managers comprised 12 percent of the total. Applying a mean turnover rate of 7.4 percent yielded annual managerial turnover of just over two hundred fifty thousand.

2. R. S. Dumbro and A. Freeman, *Seeing Tomorrow: Rewriting the Rules of Risk* (New York: John Wiley, 1998), 85.

3. Peter heard a description of this speech, given by Ash during the Ford administration, and was struck by this comment.

4. See M. Watkins, *The First 90 Days: Critical Success Strategies for New Leaders at All Levels* (Boston: Harvard Business School Press, 2003), 2–3.

Chapter 1

1. This model was originally developed in chapter 3 of M. Watkins, *The First 90 Days: Critical Success Strategies for New Leaders at All Levels* (Boston: Harvard Business School Press, 2003).

Chapter 2

1. A good summary of the earliest work on organizational change (circa 1920 onward) is provided in chapter 2 of N. M. Tichy, *Managing Strategic Change: Technical, Political, and Cultural Dynamics* (New York: John Wiley, 1983). Other important works on change management include R. Backhand and R. T. Harris, *Organizational Transitions: Managing Complex Change* (Reading, MA: Addison-Wesley, 1977); C. Argyris and D. A. Schön, *Organizational Learning: A Theory of Action Perspective* (Reading, MA: Addison-Wesley, 1978); M. Beer, *Organizational Change and Development: A Systems View* (Santa Monica, CA: Goodyear, 1980); R. M. Kanter, *The Change Masters* (New York: Simon and Schuster, 1983); and N. M. Tichy and M. A. Devanna, *The Transformational Leader* (New York: John Wiley, 1986). More recent useful work includes J. P. Kotter, *Leading Change* (Boston: Harvard Business School Press, 1996) and D. C. Hambrick, D. A. Nadler, and M. L. Tushman, *Navigating Change* (Boston: Harvard Business School Press, 1998).

Chapter 3

1. For an interesting exploration of the role of feedback loops and systems thinking in organizations, see chapters 4 and 5 of P. M. Senge, *The Fifth Discipline: The Art and Practice of the Learning Organization* (New York: Doubleday, 1990).

2. For a fascinating discussion of blocks to learning, see C. Argyris, "Teaching Smart People How to Learn," *Harvard Business Review*, May–June 1991.

3. Although the technical, political, and cultural framework appears in many of Noel Tichy's publications, the most comprehensive theoretical statement is given in *Managing Strategic Change: Technical, Political, and Cultural Dynamics* (New York: John Wiley, 1983).

4. In his work *Organizational Culture and Leadership*, Edgar Schein developed a useful framework for analyzing culture on three levels—artifacts, norms, and assumptions. *Artifacts* are the visible signs that differentiate one culture from another, including symbols such as national flags, anthems, and styles of dress. *Norms* are shared rules that guide "right behavior"—for example, modes of greeting and eating, and appropriate conduct for people at different levels in the social hierarchy. *Assumptions* are the deeper, often unspoken, beliefs that infuse and underpin social systems. Schein refers to these levels as representing "the degree to which the cultural phenomenon is visible to the observer . . . [which can] range from the very tangible overt manifestations that one can see and feel to the deeply embedded, unconscious basic assumptions . . . [that are] the essence of culture." See E. H. Schein, *Organizational Culture and Leadership*, 2nd ed. (San Francisco: Jossey-Bass, 1992), 17. See also M. T. Trice and J. M. Beyer, *The Cultures of Work Organizations* (Englewood Cliffs, NJ: Prentice-Hall, 1993).

5. For a comprehensive look at the process of best-practice benchmarking, see R. C. Camp, *Benchmarking: The Search for Industry Best Practices That Lead to Superior Performance* (Milwaukee, WI: Quality Press, 1989) and C. E. Bogan and M. J. English, *Benchmarking for Best Practices: Winning Through Innovative Adaptation* (New York: McGraw-Hill, 1994).

6. Carl Rogers and Richard Farson put it as follows: "The kind of listening we have in mind is called 'active listening.' It is called 'active' because the listener has a very definitive responsibility. He does not passively absorb words which are spoken to him. He actively tries to grasp the facts and the feelings in what he hears, and he tries, by his listening, to help the speaker work out his own problems." See C. R. Rogers and R. E. Farson, "Active Listening," in *The Organizational Behavior Reader*, 5th ed., ed. D. A. Kolb, I. R. Rubin, and J. O. Osland (Englewood Cliffs, NJ: Prentice-Hall, 1991), 187–198. See also C. Rogers and F. J. Roethlisberger, "Barriers and Gateways to Communication," *Harvard Business Review*, July–August 1952 (reissued November–December 1991).

7. David Kolb and Roger Fry developed an experiential learning model tied to stages of cognitive development. They conceived learning as a cycle consist-

ing of four stages: concrete experience, reflective observation, abstract conceptualization, and active experimentation. To be maximally effective, people need all four capabilities. But Kolb and Fry posited that these capabilities represented preferences or styles on two scales: the concrete-experience–abstract-conceptualization scale and the active-experimentation–reflective-observation scale.

Chapter 4

1. Amy Edmondson, a former colleague of Michael's at the Harvard Business School, developed this very useful distinction.

2. See J. Gabarro, *The Dynamics of Taking Charge* (Boston: Harvard Business School Press, 1987).

Chapter 6

1. See R. Heifetz, *Leadership Without Easy Answers* (Cambridge, MA: Belknap Press, 1994).

2. For an early discussion of the role of dominant coalitions in the allocation of resources and maintenance of control in organizations, see J. G. March, "The Business Firm as a Political Coalition," *Journal of Politics* 24 (1962), 662–678. More recently, John Kotter focused on the process of coalition building in *Leading Change* (Boston: Harvard Business School Press, 1996). See also J. Pfeffer, *Managing with Power: Politics and Influence in Organizations* (Boston: Harvard Business School Press, 1992).

3. See G. Egan, *Working the Shadow Side: A Guide to Positive Behind-the-Scenes Management* (San Francisco: Jossey-Bass, 1994). The shadow organization is more commonly called the "informal organization." Chester Barnard was the first to elaborate upon the distinction between formal and informal organizations. Barnard was strongly influenced by the research of Fritz Roethlisberger, especially the Hawthorne experiments, which ended up exploring the impact of informal relationship networks on organizational behavior (see F. J. Roethlisberger and W. J. Dickson, *Management and the Worker* [Cambridge, MA: Harvard University Press, 1939]). Barnard also cites Mary Parker Follett for "her great insight into the dynamic elements of organizations" (see H. C. Metcalf and L. Urwick, eds., *Dynamic Administration: The Collected Papers of Mary Parker Follett* [New York: Harper, 1940], 22). See also D. Krackhardt and J. R. Hanson, "Informal Networks: The Company Behind the Chart," *Harvard Business Review*, July–August 1993.

4. A seminal early discussion of sources of power, including information, expertise, and social influence, can be found in J. R. French and B. Raven, "The Bases of Social Power," in *Group Dynamics: Research and Theory*, eds. D. Cartwright and A. Zander (New York: Harper & Row, 1960). See also R. M. Kanter, *The Change Masters* (New York: Simon and Schuster, 1983), in which Kanter notes, "The enterprise required of innovating managers and professionals, then, is not the creative spark of genius that invents a new idea, but

rather the skill with which they move outside the formal bonds of their job, maneuvering through and around the organization in sometimes risky, unique, and novel ways . . . Organizational genius is 10 percent inspiration and 90 percent acquisition—acquisition of power to move beyond a formal job charter and to influence others . . . [O]rganizational power derives from supplies of three 'basic commodities' that can be invested in action: *information* (data, technical knowledge, political intelligence, expertise); *resources* (funds, materials, space, staff, time); and *support* (endorsement, backing, approval, legitimacy)." For a comprehensive treatment of sources of power in organizations, see chapters 4–9 of Pfeffer, *Managing with Power.*

5. The opening line of Tolstoy's *Anna Karenina* is: "Happy families are all alike; every unhappy family is unhappy in its own way."

6. This section draws extensively from chapter 4 of D. Ciampa and M. Watkins, *Right from the Start: Taking Charge in a New Leadership Role* (Boston: Harvard Business School Press, 1999).

7. This section draws extensively from chapter 7 of D. Ciampa and M. Watkins, *Right from the Start.* See also chapter 4 in D. Ciampa, *Total Quality: A User's Guide for Implementation* (Reading, MA: Addison-Wesley, 1991).

8. This connection between an impactful vision and core values comes from an unpublished paper written by David Berlew when he was running Situation Management Systems, a consulting organization located in Plymouth, MA.

9. For discussions of reasons why people resist change and approaches for dealing with them, see P. Lawrence, "How to Deal with Resistance to Change," *Harvard Business Review,* January–February 1969; R. M. Kanter "Managing the Human Side of Change," in *The Organizational Behavior Reader,* 5th ed., eds. D. A. Kolb, I. R. Rubin, and J. O. Osland (Englewood Cliffs, NJ: Prentice-Hall, 1991), 662–673; and J. P. Kotter and L. A. Schlesinger, "Choosing Strategies for Change," *Harvard Business Review,* March–April 1979.

10. See D. Lax and J. Sebenius, "Thinking Coalitionally," in *Negotiation Analysis,* ed. P. Young (Ann Arbor: University of Michigan Press, 1991) and J. Sebenius, "Sequencing to Build Coalitions: With Whom Should I Talk First?" in *Wise Choices: Decisions, Games, and Negotiations,* eds. R. Zeckhauser, R. Keeney, and J. Sebenius (Boston: Harvard Business School Press, 1996).

Chapter 7

1. This is a variation on the well-known McKinsey 7-S Model. See J. Bradach, "Organizational Alignment: The 7-S Model," Note 497045 (Boston: Harvard Business School, 1996).

2. For a seminal discussion of open systems organizational theory, see chapters 1–3 in James D. Thompson, *Organizations in Action* (New York: McGraw-Hill, 1967).

3. For more on organizational changes at the Internal Revenue Service, see C. O. Rossotti, *Many Unhappy Returns: One Man's Quest to Turn Around the*

Most Unpopular Organization in America (Boston: Harvard Business School Press, 2005).

Chapter 8

1. This chapter draws extensively on work that Michael did with Max Bazerman for their book *Predictable Surprises: The Disasters You Should See Coming and How to Avoid Them* (Boston: Harvard Business School Press, 2004), especially chapter 5, for which Michael was the primary author. Michael also originally coined the term *predictable surprises* in material for the corporate diplomacy course he taught at the Harvard Business School from 2000 to 2004.

Chapter 9

1. This concept was originally developed as a model of anxiety. See R. M. Yerkes and J. D. Dodson, "The Relation of Strength of Stimulus to Rapidity of Habit Formation," *Journal of Comparative Neurology and Psychology* 18 (1908): 459–482. Naturally, this model has limitations and is most useful as a metaphor.

2. For a discussion of "going to the balcony" in the context of negotiation, see chapter 1 of W. Ury, *Getting Past No* (New York: Bantam Doubleday, 1993).

3. See W. C. Kim and R. Mauborgne, "Fair Process: Managing in the Knowledge Economy," *Harvard Business Review,* July–August 1997, 65–75.

Recommended Reading

Managing in Public Organizations

Allison, Graham T. *Essence of Decision: Explaining the Cuban Missile Crisis.* Boston: Little Brown, 1971

Barzelay, Michael. *Breaking Through Bureaucracy: A New Vision for Managing in Government.* Berkeley, CA: University of California Press, 1992.

Heymann, Phillip B. *Politics of Public Management.* New Haven, CT: Yale University Press, 1987.

Moore, Mark Harrison. *Creating Public Value: Strategic Management in Government.* Cambridge, MA: Harvard University Press, 1996.

Moss, David A. *When All Else Fails: Government as the Ultimate Risk Manager.* Cambridge, MA: Harvard University Press, 2004.

Osborne, David, and Ted Gaebler. *Reinventing Government: How the Entrepreneurial Spirit Is Transforming the Public Sector.* New York: Penguin, 1993.

Sparrow, Malcolm. *The Regulatory Craft: Controlling Risks, Solving Problems and Managing Compliance.* Washington, DC: Brookings Institution Press, 2000.

Watkins, Michael, Mickey Edwards, and Usha Thakrar. *Winning the Influence Game: What Every Business Leader Should Know About Government.* New York: Wiley, 2001.

Making Transitions

Ciampa, Dan, and Michael Watkins. *Right from the Start. Taking Charge in a New Leadership Role.* Boston: Harvard Business School Press, 1999.

Gabarro, John J. *The Dynamics of Taking Charge.* Boston: Harvard Business School Press, 1987.

Hill, Linda A. *Becoming a Manager: How New Managers Master the Challenges of Leadership.* Boston: Harvard Business School Press, 2003.

Leadership Transitions. CD-ROM. Harvard Business School Publishing, 2004.

Crafting Strategy

Bazerman, Max H., and Michael D. Watkins. *Predictable Surprises: The Disasters You Should Have Seen Coming and How to Avoid Them.* Boston: Harvard Business School Press, 2004.

Brandenberger, Adam M., and Barry J. Nalebuff. *Co-opetition.* New York: Doubleday, 1998.

Dixit, Avinash K. and Barry J. Nalebuff. *Thinking Strategically: The Competitive Edge in Business, Politics and Everyday Life.* New York: W.W. Norton, 1993.

Porter, Michael E. *On Competition.* Boston: Harvard Business School Press, 1998.

Designing Organizations

Galbraith, Jay R. *Designing Organizations: An Executive Guide to Strategy, Structure, and Process.* San Francisco: Jossey-Bass, 2002.

Kaplan, Robert S., and David P. Norton. *The Strategy-Focused Organization: How Balanced Scorecard Companies Thrive in the New Business Environment.* Boston: Harvard Business School Press, 2000.

Nadler, David A., Michael L. Tushman, and Mark B. Nadler. *Competing by Design: The Power of Organizational Architecture.* Oxford: Oxford University Press, 1997.

Making Decisions

Bazerman, Max H. *Judgment in Managerial Decision Making.* Hoboken, NJ: John Wiley & Sons, 2005.

Hammond, John S., Ralph L. Keeney, and Howard Raiffa. *Smart Choices: A Practical Guide to Making Better Decisions.* New York: Broadway Books, 2002.

Roberto, Michael. *Why Great Leaders Don't Take Yes for an Answer: Managing for Conflict and Consensus.* Upper Saddle River, NJ: Pearson Education, 2005.

Managing Change

Bossidy, Larry, and Ram Charan. *Execution: The Discipline of Getting Things Done.* New York: Crown Publishing Group, 2002.

Kotter, John P. *Leading Change.* Boston: Harvard Business School Press, 1996.

Schein, Edgar. *Organizational Culture and Leadership,* 2nd ed. San Francisco: Jossey-Bass, 1992.

Senge, Peter M. *The Fifth Discipline: The Art & Practice of the Learning Organization.* New York: Doubleday, 1994.

Tushman, Michael L., and Charles A. O'Reilly III. *Winning Through Innovation: A Practical Guide to Leading Organizational Change and Renewal.* Boston: Harvard Business School Press, 2002.

Negotiating and Persuading

Burley-Allen, Madelyn. *Listening: The Forgotten Skill.* New York: John Wiley & Sons, 1995.

Cialdini, Robert B. *Influence: The Psychology of Persuasion.* New York: William Morrow & Company, 1993.

Fisher, Roger, William Ury, and Bruce Patton. *Getting to Yes: Negotiating Agreement Without Giving In.* New York: Penguin, 1991.

Stone, Douglas, Bruce Patton, and Sheila Heen. *Difficult Conversations: How to Discuss What Matters Most.* New York: Penguin, 2000.

Ury, William. *Getting Past No: Negotiating Your Way from Confrontation to Coopera-tion.* New York: Bantam, 1993.

Leading and Team Building

Heifetz, Ronald A., and Marty Linsky. *Leadership on the Line: Staying Alive Through the Dangers of Leading.* Boston: Harvard Business School Press, 2003.

Katzenbach, Jon R., and Douglas K. Smith. *The Wisdom of Teams: Creating the High-Performance Organization.* New York: HarperCollins, 2003.

Kayser, Thomas A. *Building Team Power: How to Unleash the Collaborative Genius of Work Teams.* New York: McGraw-Hill, 1994.

Index

About the Authors

Peter H. Daly had a thirty-three-year career in the federal government, beginning as a management intern, progressing through supervisory and middle-management ranks, and spending the last eighteen years of his career as a member of the Senior Executive Service. He served as CEO of two U.S. Treasury agencies and led U.S. delegations to monetary conferences in almost every region of the world. He chaired a fourteen-nation research consortium, consulted for several foreign governments, served in Russia and Eastern Europe with the Financial Services Volunteer Corps, and was appointed to a presidential commission to study various counterterrorism issues. He volunteered as Chairman of the Board for Grandma's Houses, a group of not-for-profit facilities in Washington, D.C., that care for abused, neglected, indigent, or otherwise at-risk children and for the elderly. Since leaving government service, he has served as a national security consultant to Booz Allen Hamilton and published two research studies under the aegis of the Harvard Program on Information Resources Policy. He holds a bachelor's degree in economics from Villanova University.

Michael Watkins is a Professor of Practice at INSEAD, the leading European business school, and the founding partner of Genesis Advisers, a leadership strategy consultancy. He is the author of *The First 90 Days: Critical Success Strategies for New Leaders at all Levels* and coauthor of *Right from the Start: Taking Charge in a New Leadership Role* and *Predictable Surprises: The Disasters You Should Have Seen Coming and How to Prevent Them*, which was a *Strategy+Business* best business book of 2004. He is also the author of several books on negotiation and many articles, which have appeared in such publications as *Harvard Business Review, Sloan Management Review, Leadership Quarterly, Executive Update,* and *Negotiation Journal.* Between 1991 and 1996, he was a professor at the Kennedy School of Government. From 1996 to 2003, he was a professor at the Harvard Business School. He received a degree in electrical engineering from the University of Waterloo, did graduate work in law and business at the University of Western Ontario, and completed his PhD in decision sciences at Harvard University.

Cate Reavis is a freelance casewriter and consultant. Her clients include Genesis Advisers (for whom she has developed a series of case studies on public-sector leadership transitions), the Kennedy School of Government, and North-eastern University's School of Management. From 1997 to 2004, she was a se-nior researcher at the Harvard Business School where she coauthored over fifty case studies with twenty-five faculty members from all academic units, con-ducted hundreds of interviews with senior executives and organizational lead-ers, and traveled extensively throughout Europe, Asia, and Africa. From August 1995 to September 1996, she was the manager of operations at Eaton Consult-ing, a Boston-based cross-cultural training and consulting firm. She holds a BA in international relations and Spanish from Lake Forest College, and an MA in international policy studies from the Monterey Institute of International Stud-ies in Monterey, California.